FRESHWATER
FISHING
1000 TIPS FROM THE PROS

FRESHWATER FISHING

1000 TIPS FROM THE PROS

HENRY WASZCZUK
& ITALO LABIGNAN

KEY PORTER BOOKS

Canadian Cataloguing in Publication Data

Waszczuk, Henry, 1950-
　　　　Freshwater fishing: 1000 tips from the pros

ISBN: 1-55013-453-1

1. Fishing.　2. Freshwater fishes. I. Labignan, Italo, 1955- . II. Title.

SH441.W38 1992　　799.1'1　　C92-095709-9

Key Porter Books
70 The Esplanade
Toronto, Ontario
Canada M5E 1R2

Illustrations: Joe Hartnett, Sheilagh Mercer and Chuck Weiss
Photographs: Colin Clarke Photography, p. 182; Al Fraser, p.125 (top), p. 131; Mark Fraser, p. 125 (bottom); P. Hartman, p. 54; JL Photo, p.147; Bruce Johnstone, p. 124; Jocelyn Lapointe, p. 63; Gene Lopushinsky, p. 169; David Morgan, p. 17 (right); Cam Nevitt, p. 99; Mike Pade, p. 66; Jim Pierdon, p. 62; Kevin Rice, p. 70; Gary Storoschuk, p. 162; John Summerfield, p. 13, 17 (left), 127; Mark Tarnawczyk, p. 140.

The first aid information in this book is not intended to take the place of a medical doctor's advice.

Cover photograph of Italo Labignan (left) and Henry Waszczuk (right): Canadian Sportfishing Productions

Printed and bound in the United States of America

94 95 96 97 98 6 5 4 3 2

Contents

Preface

During our many years of fishing in all parts of the world, we've had the good fortune to become familiar with a large number of fish species. On these trips for our television shows, books, and magazine articles, we've gathered the more than 1,000 tips that are featured in this book.

We believe that anyone can learn the art of successful fishing with the right information. Whether you're a bass fisherman, a trolling enthusiast, or an ice fisherman, *Freshwater Fishing* has been written to give you that extra edge which helps the pros win tournaments.

Many of these tips were generously donated by fellow anglers. Our thanks are extended to these unnamed sportsmen who did not hesitate to pass on their expertise. We would also like to extend our thanks to Sheilagh Mercer, Chuck Weiss and Joe Hartnett for their illustrations; Charlie McDonald for his help in coordinating the project; and our corporate sponsors in the boating and fishing industry who have supported this book.

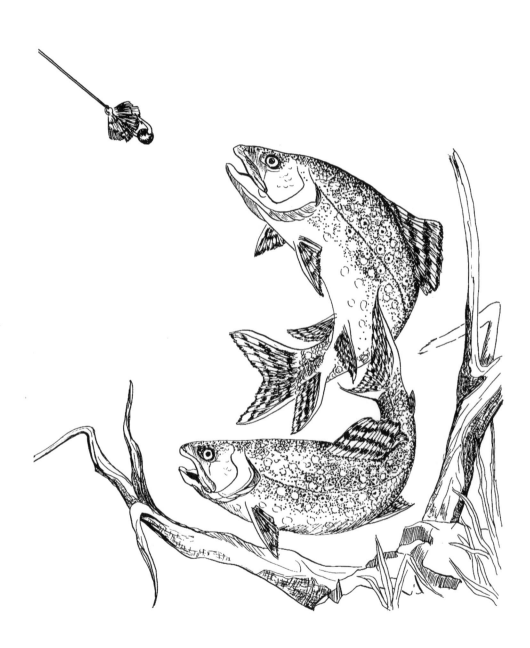

General Fishing Tips

Freshwater fishing continues to be one of the world's most popular outdoor activities, and with good reason. It is a relatively inexpensive sport — a good quality rod and reel and a supply of artificial lures may cost as little as $75 — and it provides limitless hours of enjoyment.

Over the years, anglers have found that by using certain techniques, they can catch more fish in a shorter period of time. Regardless of what your favorite species may be or where you fish, the following tips are intended to provide you with general information that will help you become a better angler.

BEFORE YOU
GO FISHING

- If you are a beginner angler, don't buy a lot of equipment and tackle. Start out with one rod and reel outfit and a small assortment of lures that will catch fish in your area. To find out what to buy, check with a local fishing club member or knowledgeable friends.

- To save money on equipment, look at catalogues from several outlets and make a comparative price list of items that you normally buy, such as reels, rods, and tackle.

- Ninety percent of the tackle on the market is designed to catch the fisherman rather than the fish. Shop for tackle with the type of fish you want to catch in mind. Don't buy every lure you see; select lures on their own merits, not by their package design and description.

- Every angler who has tried to keep a fishing log while out on the water knows how difficult it can be to take the time to write everything down — especially if the fish are biting. A great way to simplify the process is to carry a miniature tape recorder strapped to your belt.

While you're fishing, record information such as location, lures used, methods of presentation, and weather conditions. When you get home, you can easily transcribe the recorded information into your personal fishing log.

- Anglers sometimes go overboard when buying lures. It's more important to have a wide range of different colored lures in your tackle box than a large number of different types of lures. Buy only a few varieties of the better-known lures and use color prism tape to make a color change.

- When using laminated hydrographic maps, mark your hot spots with a grease pencil. Use a green pencil to mark weed lines that might change from year to year, a yellow pencil to mark potential hot spots, and a red pencil to mark confirmed hot spots. But remember, don't let other anglers catch a glimpse of your map.

- You never know when matches will come in handy. To insure that they'll always work, use the wooden kind, waterproof them by coating the heads with nail polish, and store them in a waterproof container.

To make a lanyard to hold your sunglasses or your line clippers, first buy about 18 inches (45 cm) of heavy monofilament line in about 25- to 30-pound test. For your line clippers, pass the line through the hole in the clippers and secure the two ends of line with electrical sleeves. For your sunglasses, tie the monofilament line around the arms of the glasses and seal the knots by melting them with a match.

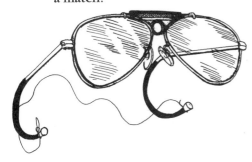

Many of us know that certain scents repel fish. To avoid this, keep a bottle of Dr. Juice Hand & Lure Cleaner or some Berkley Erase on hand. These products will remove oily deposits or human scent from your lures. You can also use them to remove the fishy smell on your hands after you've cleaned a mess of fish for the table.

Don't let your fishing trip be ruined by a broken spring in your casting reel. Save the little springs from your worn-out ball-point pens and carry several in your tackle box. They can be easily modified to fit and work in your reel.

Most boat anglers carry a small tool kit in their boat, but how many toss in a tube of Super Glue, a couple of extra rod tips, some line wrap, and maybe some clear nail polish or winding finish? There's nothing worse than losing the tip off your favorite rod. Be ready to make this on-the-water repair to save some valuable fishing time.

Polarized sunglasses are a must when fishing. Yellow or amber lenses are great for cloudy or dull days, while dark lenses should be worn on sunny days and when ice fishing. In the winter, reflection from the snow can tire you out. In the summer, wearing sunglasses allows you to see the fish before they see you.

Many anglers are not aware of the potential danger of cold winds and water in remote areas. Hypothermia, a condition caused by the chilling of the inner core of the body, can result in mental and physical collapse. Pay close attention to the wind chill factor and dress accordingly.

Perspiring or cold feet can be uncomfortable on a fishing trip. Always carry an extra pair of socks on hot or cold days.

To stay warm while fishing throughout the winter months, wear outerwear containing goose down.

If you're fishing in strong winds or cold rain, apply a thin base of petroleum jelly to your face. It will help prevent chapping and cracked lips.

Over a period of time, your luncheon cooler and/or thermos can smell musty. This can be eliminated by cleaning them with a solution of water and a couple of spoonfuls of baking soda. Rinse a few times with clean water.

Water frozen in a plastic jug keeps food cold in your cooler and, as it melts, can provide you with a thirst-quenching drink. For a change, try freezing lemonade or fruit juice.

FISHING TECHNIQUES

Don't release live baitfish into waters other than those from which they were originally taken. It is illegal and can seriously damage the fishery.

Fan casting is the most productive fishing technique whether you're casting from shores, piers, or boats. Don't repeat casts to an area unless you have had a follow from a fish.

Fishing is best under these conditions: on slightly overcast days, in the morning or late evening, where the water is slightly discolored, and in heavy cover areas.

When traveling in a fishing boat, especially in rough water, don't hook your lure into your guides or the rod tip. This will not only damage your guides but will also increase the risk of tangles. Just hook your lure onto the bail of your spinning rod or the line guide bar on your baitcasting rod.

 If you don't have any steel leaders with you, connect several snap-swivels together. They will form a temporary leader.

 If you have to use a snap-swivel or leader, use black rather than silver. Black is almost invisible even in the clearest water, whereas silver is extremely noticeable.

 The larger the lure, the bigger the odds of hooking a large fish. Some fish such as muskies and pike have been known to attack fish of their own size.

 If you're having trouble finding fish, try fishing parallel to weed lines and casting into open pockets in the weeds.

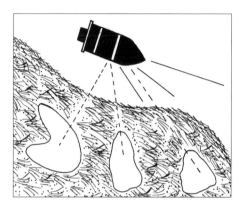

 Try these five tips for better casting:
• A thinner line casts better.
• Don't overfill your reel.
• Line up the target area and keep

your eye on it continually.
- Watch your backswing and follow through. Don't go farther back than 10 o'clock.
- Casting is all in the wrist. Control your cast; don't muscle it.

◀ Short staking is an excellent technique to keep the fish from getting its head down and diving. Just use some short lifting strokes as well as some quick pumping action on your rod. Your landing percentage should improve.

◀ Anglers who spend a lot of time on the water casting spinnerbaits, crankbaits, and other lures are often affected by forearm and elbow pain — similar to tennis elbow. An easy way to relieve the stress on your joints and arm muscles is to switch to a casting rod with a longer butt section for two-handed casting. You won't believe the difference it makes.

◀ Pattern fishing consists of seeking out certain combinations of conditions such as weather, water temperature, water clarity, and underwater structures that have been successful for you in the past. No matter where you go, the pattern should work for you again and again.

◀ Drifting is a favorite technique used by anglers for many species of fish. If your boat is drifting too fast over weed beds and shoals, tie a plastic pail to a strong line attached to the boat. The drag can be altered by adjusting the amount of rope you let out.

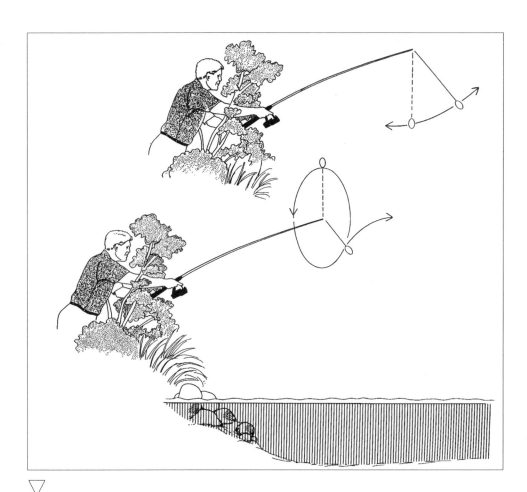

When shoreline trees and brush impede your ability to cast properly, especially along the banks of small streams, try an underhand pendulum-style flip cast or a circular cast.

Night-fishing results can be improved by using a fluorescent line and a small black light. A second light choice would be a flashlight or a light rigged to a hat such as those used by miners.

When using a float with bait, ideally you should weight the line below the float with just enough sinkers to keep the float up. This way you will see the slightest tap and the fish will feel the least resistance when the float starts to sink below the surface.

In choppy water conditions, fish along the windward shore. Your body and the boat will be partially concealed from the fish because rough water distorts their vision.

- Most species of fish prefer a specific water temperature at different times of the year. If you own a temperature probe, you can use it to find fish at whatever depth offers this specific temperature.

AFTER THE CATCH

- A handy way to measure fish is to mount a measuring stick on one of your boat seats or even on the floor of your boat. No more misplaced measuring tapes. You can quickly measure your fish, then let them go.

- When you are putting a fish on a stringer, never put the stringer through its gills. Always pass it through the thin membrane of the lower jaw. This area is strong enough to ensure that the fish will not rip off the stringer.

- The size, shape, and color of your quarry's prey should be imitated as closely as possible. Check the contents of the stomach of the fish you decide to keep. If, for example, a walleye has a couple of crayfish in its digestive tract, you should use live crayfish or crayfish-colored lures.

- Every province and state has its own fishing regulations, sport fishing licenses, enforcement laws, and catch and size limits. Take heed and be a true sportfisherman.

- If you land a government-tagged fish, forward the tag to the address on the tag along with the following information: your name, address, the species of fish, its length and weight, and where and when it was caught.

- Before you travel home, clean any fish that you've kept and store them in a cool place in your vehicle. If you do not have a cooler, use newspaper and large ferns or leaves to insulate your fish. Don't place fish whole in a closed plastic bag. This will raise the inside temperature even more, and the liquid in the digestive tract of the fish may taint the meat.

TAKING CHILDREN FISHING

- Don't get up too early or stay out too late. It's better to end the day with the children wanting to continue, rather than having them go home too tired.

Pick a fishing spot with plenty of casting room and away from the crowds, especially if you are fishing from the bank. On a lake, avoid areas that have too many hang-ups on the bottom.

Don't over-coach. The first-time angler will do better if you let him or her make some mistakes, before pointing out how they can be corrected.

Stress catch and release, but remember that first-timers are especially proud of their catch. Let them show off their prizes.

Choose lures that won't be lost easily; for example, spinner-baits are great for bass, while weedless lures are effective for most fish in shallow, weedy waters.

Take some snacks with you and make sure that you take numerous breaks if the fishing is slow. Enjoy the scenery around you.

Don't take your best equipment. Secondary gear will prevent you from fishing too seriously and, if anything does get broken, little harm has been done.

Tackle

on't be fooled into buying tackle just to get by. It's no fun fighting a heavyweight fish on ultralight gear or a featherweight on a heavy-action outfit. Learn to match your tackle to the fish, the reel to the rod, the rod to the line, and the line to the lure. If you follow this advice, you will not only become more proficient in catching fish, but you will also probably land the bigger ones that usually slip away.

With the high price of tackle these days, storage and care have become very important. Far too many fishermen don't take proper care of their tackle, then go on a fishing trip only to find their reels, lures, and other tackle in poor condition. The following tips relating to tackle care will save you time, money, and, most of all, headaches.

LINES

If your fishing line appears chalky – a powdery residue comes off the line – it means it is starting to deteriorate and should be replaced.

At times it is very difficult to pick out frayed areas on your line by simply passing the line through your hand. Passing the line through your lips, however, makes it easier to feel wear spots.

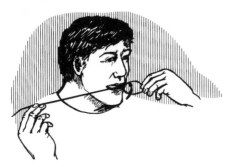

To save line, empty your spool when the line becomes worn and reel it on the opposite way; this will let you use that portion of your line that was previously buried and unused.

Old line can become brittle. When purchasing fishing line, check the date of manufacture or ask the store attendant if the line has been stocked recently. Always purchase the "freshest" line possible.

When loading a spool with fresh line, it's important to fill your reel properly. Ask a friend to help. To prevent line twists on spinning reels, always fill the reel directly from the manufacturer's line spool, which should be held with a pencil. For baitcasting reels, the spool should be held in the same manner. Be sure not to set the tension on the incoming line with your fingers as this may cause line twist. Always set the tension on the line being spooled by having the person holding the pencil put pressure on the sides of the new line spool.

Always lubricate your knot with saliva or water as you are tightening it. This will make the knot much tighter and will reduce the chance of the knot weakening from friction.

Doubling the line to tie the knot doesn't necessarily make the knot stronger. In fact, it can weaken it. It's much better to tie one of the stronger knots on a single line.

If you have trouble poking your line through the eye of a hook, buy a needle threader for about 50 cents at a store that sells sewing supplies. It does a quick and easy job.

Even top-rated knots fail when tied incorrectly or hurriedly. Remember, avoid twisting the line, pull loops slowly, wet the line, and pull all knots tight. Here are a few knots for you to memorize and master.

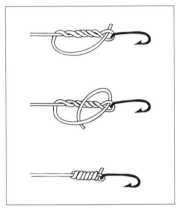

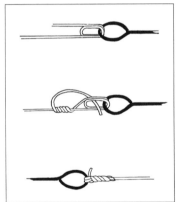

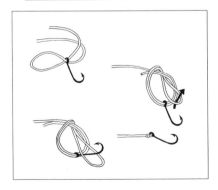

When trimming a knot, always leave ⅛ inch (25 mm) of line as a lead. If the knot starts to slip a little, it won't come undone.

Be careful with sections of unwanted monofilament. Birds, animals, and even motors suffer from carelessly discarded line. The best place to dispose of it is in the rubbish can or, if you're on a long backpacking trip, you can melt it in the fire. Berkley has a line-recycling program; you can dispose of your line at most tackle stores in a special recycling bin.

A knot should be retied whenever six or more fish have been landed, especially fish with pronounced teeth, such as muskies and pike.

Never tighten a knot with your fingernails. To prevent nicks, always use the inside of your fingertips to draw the knot tight.

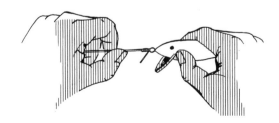

➤ Some people add lubricants to their monofilament line to make it pass over their guides more smoothly. Others add chemicals to keep their guides from freezing in cold weather. Before you use these products, check the packaging to make sure that what you are using won't damage your fishing line, and also be aware that those foreign scents on your line can repel fish.

➤ When fishing in shallow, rocky, or stump-filled water, always check the last 3 to 5 feet (90 to 150 cm) of line for nicks or scrapes. Line that is in constant contact with rough bottom structure can be weakened by as much as 90 percent.

➤ The best way to take the twist out of fishing line is to remove your lure and trail the line behind your boat at a moderate speed. Try to let out as much line as possible.

➤ When you have several reels, it often helps to record which line strength you have on each reel. Using a pencil, simply write the type and strength of the line on the spool of your spinning reel and on the side of the housing if you have a bait-caster.

➤ Here's an easy way to check if your fishing line is set for battle. Tie an overhand knot and determine whether it cuts the line under reasonable pressure. If it does, move up your line and test again until the line holds. Trim off the weak fragments.

➤ Whenever you are using light line of less than 6-pound test, you should take extreme care when adding any terminal tackle to the line. Floats should be held to the line with rubber tubing rather than wire springs or knots.

➤ Whenever you want to move sinkers up or down your line, whether they're split shot, twist, or bell sinkers, you should remove them from the line and then reattach them to the desired position. Sliding the sinkers up or down can weaken the line. If you must slide them, wet the line first to reduce friction and damage to the line.

➤ Always store fishing line in a dark, cool, dry place away from chemicals and other toxic substances. Many people mistakenly store their fishing rods and reels along with their outboard motor and gas tank in a garage or storage shed. The best place to store your line is in a closet.

- To prevent line damage, split shot sinkers should be squeezed onto the line with your fingers rather than pliers or teeth.

- When fishing very clear water, a lighter leader may be used to increase the "naturalness" of the presentation. For example, if you have 8-pound test line on your reel, use a swivel to attach a length of 2- or 4-pound test line about 2 feet (60 cm) long. Your hook and other terminal tackle can then be attached carefully to the leader.

- Fluorescent line has its useful moments in the late evening, at night, and in murky waters, but remember, if you can see it so can the fish. High-visibility lines spook fish in normal conditions.

- To prevent your line from breaking when you're fighting a fish, make sure that the reel's drag is not set too tightly. A good rule of thumb is to set the drag at half the pound-breaking strength of the line. Make sure you test your drag by pulling the line all the way through your rod guides and not just a few inches (several centimetres) from your reel face. Tie the line to a stationary object, put a bend in the rod, and apply full drag. Then loosen the drag until you can back away easily with the rod tip bent.

- Never store spare monofilament line in the sun. Ultraviolet rays will not only shorten its useful life, but may also cause it to break more readily under the strain of a trophy fish.

LURES

- A great lure organizer that you can mount anywhere in your boat is a toothbrush holder. They often come with a self-adhesive backing, making them a handy way to keep your favorite lures close at hand.

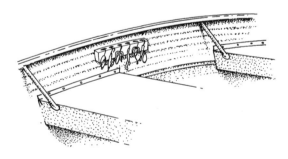

- When using wobbling lures, always use a snap or a loose knot like the Rapala knot, which allows the lure to operate freely. If a wobbling lure is not working properly or is riding on its side, it may be that the knot is restricting the action of the lure.

- Styrofoam or cork strips attached to your aluminum boat's gunwale can make ideal spots to hang and dry your lures before storing them in your tackle box.

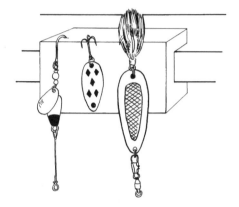

- Quality not quantity is what counts when it comes to buying lures. Buy the best you can afford.

- It really pays to stick with brand name plastic lures. Many lures that prove to be immensely successful, such as the Mister Twister Sassy Shad, are often copied; however, the copies are rarely as good. Most don't have the same "fish-catching" action.

- Large lures can be difficult to store in an average-sized tackle box. Here's an inexpensive solution. Purchase a Styrofoam cooler; push the hooks into the top edges, letting the lures lie along the inner walls.

- Great sales can be found near the end of the fishing season. This is the best time to purchase top-quality fishing tackle.

- When using spinning lures such as spinners, spoons, or jigs, always tie a swivel 10 to 14 inches (25 to 35 cm) up the line to prevent line twisting. Snap swivels should be as small as possible. Swivels with ball bearings are much more efficient than standard swivels. Two high-quality ball bearing swivels are Berkley Lock snap-swivels and Sampo swivels.

- A lure with a sound chamber works well in "stained" water. Sometimes a little noise will wake up those lunkers.

- Pork rind is an effective bait for many fish species, but it's not cheap. In order to reuse it, it's necessary to keep the pork rind from drying out. You can either wrap your pig'n'jig in a wet sponge or cloth or you can store it in a small plastic container.

- Several battery-operated hook sharpeners are on the market. They are compact and powerful and will last most of the fishing season on a couple of C-size batteries.

- Keep several pieces of color prism tape in your tackle box. This little addition will reduce the number of lures you need to buy. When the fish start hitting a certain color, just apply the appropriate colored tape to any lure you want to use.

- When you are fishing "stained" water, fluorescent-colored lures will work better than lures in natural colors. Natural colors fade, whereas fluorescent colors stand out in murky or deep water.

- If you are fishing shallow, snag-filled water and are using artificial lures, change the lower (front) treble to a large single hook to decrease your odds of hanging up on the bottom. Single (Siwash) lure hooks still hook fish extremely well.

- With a little hot water and strong detergent, you can restore your plastic skirted baits and worms quite easily. Remember to take the hooks out before kneading a handful of them in the soapy water. Rinse and repeat.

- Believe it or not, an ordinary pencil eraser will remove minor rust accumulations on most chrome-plated fishing products.

- Never change the size of the trebles on an artificial lure unless you're willing to do some fine-tuning. Most artificial lures have been designed to work properly with certain sizes and weights of hooks.

- Keep hooks needle-sharp at all times. The larger the hook, the blunter it will usually be. By using a file, stone, or even one of the new electric sharpeners, you'll reduce your "misses" by at least 50 percent.

- A properly sharpened hook placed by its point on the nail of your finger will not slip off.

- You can increase the glow of phosphorescent lures used to catch salmon and many other freshwater gamefish by "charging" them with a camera flash or a powerful flashlight.

- Slight modifications to the eyelet of many lures can decrease or increase the action of the lure. Using small pliers, you can fine-tune most lures to help entice those lazy fish to bite.

- To prevent rust from forming on your lures, dry them with a hot-air hair dryer as soon as you get home.

RODS

- Sporting goods repair outlets sell unclaimed fishing tackle. You can often pick up a great deal on rods and reels for the price of repairs alone.

- Use furniture polish on your rods to keep them shiny and new. It also helps keep dirt and scratches to a minimum.

- By encircling the top edge of your rod case with your thumb  and forefinger when removing the rod, you'll prevent the rod guides and even the windings from catching the hard lip of the case and getting damaged.

- An old bottle of nail polish kept in your tackle box can come in handy. Loose or frayed rod guide windings can easily be repaired with nail polish.

- If your two-piece rod has become loose and constantly comes apart, try applying some common candle wax to the male part of the ferrule. This will produce a nice tight fit.

- When taking your rod apart, never hold on to the guides. Always hold the main blank as close to the ferrule as possible and use a twisting rather than a yanking motion to separate the pieces.

- Two-piece rods are often hard to separate. Try this. Before putting your rod together, rub a little oil over the ferrule. This lubricates the connection so the rod will separate easily when it's time to pack up.

- Many anglers put in hundreds of hours of fishing in one season. Casting fatigue will always set in at some point. To help alleviate this problem, you can sand down the cork grip to an oval shape with coarse sandpaper, followed by fine sandpaper. There's nothing like a fitted grip for comfort and ease in casting.

- Revolving your rod slowly while varnishing the rod windings helps prevent drips and runs and ensures a professional-looking overall job.

- To pick out any damaged areas on your rod guides or reel that may be ruining your line, use a cotton swab to go over each guide and tip. Pass the swab

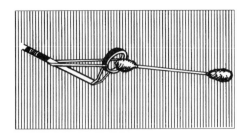

over the roller on the bail of your spinning reel or the line guide on your baitcaster. The swab will leave traces of cotton wherever there are burrs or worn areas.

REELS

- Before loading your reel with new monofilament, soak the spool of line in water for a few hours or even overnight. The line's "memory" or set will relax, and the line will transfer more easily onto your reel.

- If you want your reel to operate efficiently, don't overfill it. Leave ⅛ inch (25 mm) of space at the spool's lip. Also make sure you apply moderate tension when filling your reel.

- Reels with a trigger-line pick-up are great for casting, but for jig fishermen they can be a nuisance. All these reels have a bail that rotates freely for a quarter to half of the diameter of the spool at a time. This means that if you are not retrieving the line or casting, but jigging up and down, the bail will rotate, resulting in loose line. This may also occur when setting the hook if your hand is not on the handle.

- If monofilament line remains unused on a reel for a period of time, it can snarl, forming "birds' nests." To help eliminate this problem, soak the line for an hour or so before your next fishing excursion.

- An easy way to clear line tangles on reels is with a small crochet hook (size 4 or 6). Just store it in your tackle box of goodies.

- If your reel starts to slip in the rod's reel seat, use some electrical tape to anchor it more securely. The tape will keep your hands off the metal and you can remove it whenever you want.

- Baitcasters with "V" spools will help increase the length of your casts and decrease "birds' nests" or backlashes.

- If you want smoother and longer casts from your spinning reel, just add some car wax to the contact part of the spool's lip. Be sure to buff the wax completely.

If you drop your reel in dirt or sand, make sure to rinse it thoroughly in water as soon as possible. Abrasive material on the line can damage guides and reel parts, which in turn will result in line damage.

For continuous casting and retrieving of lures, high gear ratio reels are much better than low gear ratio reels. The gear ratio describes how many times the spool rotates for each turn of the handle. With a 5:1 gear ratio, every time you turn the handle, the spool rotates five times. A 5:1 gear ratio reel will thus pick up more line with one rotation of the reel handle than a 3.5:1 gear ratio reel.

The average fisherman never uses more than the first 60 to 80 yards (54 to 73 m) of line on a high-capacity spinning reel. To save on monofilament line, purchase an arbor to fill the back of the spool or fill the bottom of the spool with older line.

A little lubricant on reels is a good idea. Be careful, however, not to apply too much. Dirt, dust, and even sand can get trapped by excess oil. Always clean and store your reels properly, but oil them sparingly.

Spinning reels achieve much better line control and cast better with 2- to 6-pound test line, especially on windy days.

If you are an ultralight angler, you should look for the reel with the smoothest drag system. Rear reel mount drags are much easier to work than star drags located on the spools of spinning reels.

A magnetic reel will help the novice baitcaster avoid line twists or "over-runs"; however, inexpensive magnetic reels usually have oil-less bearings rather than ball bearings, and these tend to wear faster under prolonged use.

If you fish with heavier line, you may want to consider using a baitcasting reel. Baitcasting reels are ideal for trolling because of their higher line capacity and low gear ratio.

When choosing a baitcasting reel, always match the reel weight to the rod. When the outfit is held at the reel, it should feel balanced and light.

When casting with a baitcaster, the wrist, not the extended arm, should be snapping the cast out. Using the wrist will give you greater casting distance and will be less tiring. A trick that will help you learn to use your wrist is to place a pocket wallet under your casting armpit. If you drop the wallet when casting, you are using your arm. If the wallet doesn't fall, you are casting properly with your wrist.

◄ Before a baitcaster is stored, always let off the tension on the drag completely. Reels that are stored with the drag set tightly may end up with a locked drag.

MISCELLANEOUS EQUIPMENT

◄ Never leave plastic, rubber, or vinyl baits, such as worms, grubs, or skirts, in a tackle box that is not "worm proof." The different chemicals may react and damage the tackle box.

◄ The best all-around knife blade is a stainless steel one. It takes a little longer to sharpen, but it won't rust. Carbon steel blades tend to discolor over a period of time. Whatever your choice, keep the blade protected in some kind of sheath.

◄ Silicone in a tube is an excellent product to seal a hole or rip in your waders or hip boots. Make sure the rubber is dry, sand lightly to form a rough surface, then smear the silicone on the inside and outside of the damaged area. Allow the area to dry before using the waders or boots.

◄ When fishing big gamefish such as pike and musky, braided wire leaders occasionally get bent. When this happens, stretch the leader tight and rub it back and forth across your knee. The friction will heat it, realigning the leader to its original straight position.

◄ Wire leaders are great for catching muskies and pike, but for many other freshwater species the leader just deadens the action of the lure.

◄ Some tackle boxes crack after years of rough use. Don't throw them away. Apply plastic pipe joint cement to the crack, hold the crack closed while the cement bonds, and you've got yourself a working tackle box again.

◄ Cementing a sheet of sandpaper to the bottom of your sharpening stone eliminates sliding and a possible slip of the blade while sharpening.

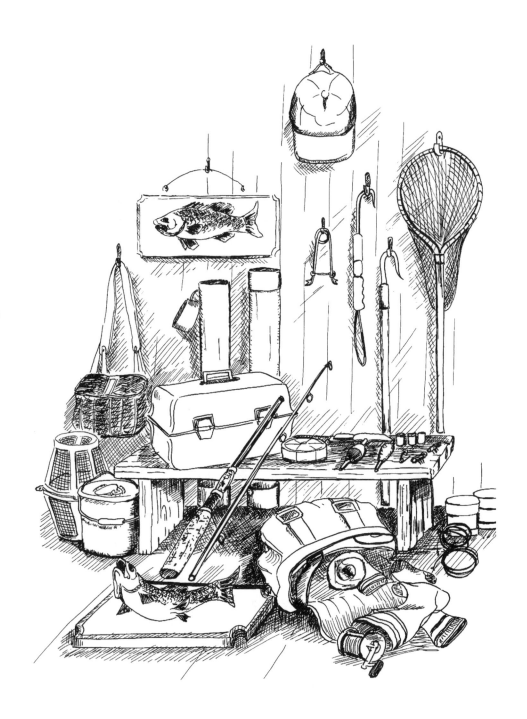

Storage

Whether you're on the road, at home, or in your boat, the storage of tackle and related gear requires some forethought and care. Most anglers are so excited about having some time to go fishing that they pack their car, boat, or knapsack in a careless way. Many rods and reels are broken or damaged because they have not been packaged properly.

On another note, when has an angler not left something behind when traveling to a favorite fishing spot? Just the use of a simple checklist can be inexpensive insurance against forgetting a piece of equipment on a fishing trip.

Over the years, manufacturers have designed unique storage compartments, satchels, and other devices to solve the problem of storage for anglers. However, the cost of these items can be prohibitive. The following hints will not only save you money but also some valuable fishing time by keeping your equipment in top shape.

• Plastic bags encourage corrosion through moisture build-up. A better method for keeping dirt and dust out of your reel machinery is to place your reels in cloth bags or wrap them in pieces of cloth using elastic bands to secure them.

• Identification tags for your fishing equipment can be easily made from expired credit cards. After cutting them down to size, just punch or drill holes in the corner of the tags. You can even reinforce the holes with grommets.

• You can easily and safely store various hooks and lures in scrap pieces of Styrofoam.

• When you're going on a major fishing trip, pack your reels in socks and place them in a carrying bag or suitcase.

• Store all fishing rods on proper rod racks in your home. Rods should stand upright. They shouldn't be left leaning against walls or lying horizontally, because they will warp if they remain in the same stressed position for months.

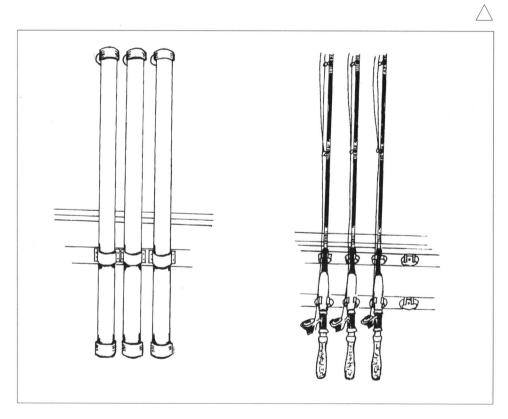

Here's a tip if you are going on a camping-fishing trip. Don't throw away that snarl of fishing line you just cut off your rod. If you wad it into a ball and tie the loose ends around the middle to keep it together, it makes a good scouring pad for the frying pan.

A leather sheath will protect your knife blade and its sharpness; however, remember to lightly oil the blade once in a while. The sheath will more than likely hold moisture that could discolor or rust it.

Garbage bags have multiple uses. One is to carry your foul-weather gear. When you return home, however, be sure to air-dry your gear to help prevent mildew and rot.

Many anglers who like to travel light use empty Sucrets metal containers to store their ultra-light lures and terminal tackle. Wrapping an elastic band around the tin will prevent it from opening in your pouch or bag.

Reels require careful maintenance. Keep them away from dirt and grime as much as possible and, after each trip, wash the reel if necessary to remove algae, dirt, and dust. On spinning reels, remove the spool and wash it separately. Treat all reels with oil or WD-40 to remove moisture and to protect moving parts.

Christmas gift-wrap tubes are ideal for storing your topographical and hydrographical maps and charts. Each tube can be marked and labeled for easy access and organization.

Elastic "bungee" straps are handy on a fishing trip. If you're fishing in a canoe, secure all your major items in case of capsizing. Simply pass the strap through the handles of your gear bags and boxes and then attach the ends to the gunwales. In the event of a mishap, you may get wet but at least you won't lose your valuable equipment.

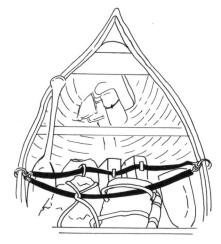

Many 35 mm film manufacturers are now making their film canisters in clear plastic. What a great place to store small tackle items such as swivels, split shots, and hooks.

Another easy way to store terminal tackle such as swivels and snaps is to place them on large safety pins. Just thread different sizes of swivels on different safety pins.

The best way to protect your hydrographical and topographical maps for life is by lamination. Another less expensive method is to cover the entire surface of the map with transparent contact sheeting, sold in most hardware departments.

Whether you're working on lures, terminal tackle, or your reel, an egg carton is handy for temporary storage and separation of parts.

You don't need to buy expensive rod cases before going on a distant fishing trip. Purchase lengths of 4-inch (10-cm) diameter PVC plastic piping, cement a cap on one end and tape a cap on the other end. These homemade cases will last forever and are much less expensive.

Save those empty margarine containers. They are usually made of non-breakable plastic and have leak-proof lids. They make great storage jars for bait.

If you want to keep fish on ice for a period of time, use blocks of ice. Block ice melts much more slowly than cubed ice. In fact, even half blocks can be used if your storage area is tight for space.

When you are traveling in a boat between fishing spots and are using live bait or pork rind, use a film container filled with water to keep the bait moist.

Simply make a hole and a slit in the lid and partially fill the container with water. Slip your bait inside, fit the line through the slit in the lid, and close the top.

🐟 A zippered pencil case is an inexpensive waterproof case to hold your wallet and fishing licenses.

🐟 Try using a 4- to 6-inch (10- to 15-cm) square Tupperware container for carrying an extra roll of graph paper, fuses, matches, and other small items in your boat. When the lid is on tightly, it is completely waterproof.

🐟 When traveling, lay your rods tip-to-butt before storing them in a tube container. You'll have fewer worries about breakage. For even more protection, you can place a wooden dowel in the tube for added strength.

🐟 Before storing reels, take the time to do these simple maintenance steps. They will give you smoother performance, longer reel life, and easier fishing:
• *Baitcasting reels* — Oil the handles and any other oil ports on the reel; grease the level wind pawl and gear.
• *Spincast reels* — Oil the handle, thumb release, and the pick-up pin inside the cap.

• *Spinning reels* — Oil the bushing under the roller and the reel handle, and use a few drops at the points where the bail attaches to the rotating cup.
• *Fly reels* — Oil the handle and spool, and the click mechanism on the inside.

🐟 If you're planning on carrying or storing several fully rigged rods together, tag your lures to the rigged reels, tighten the lines with the reels, then wrap the lines running from your rod tips to the lures several times around the rods so that they catch on the guides. This will prevent lines from crossing and tangling.

🐟 Ropes are used by anglers and boaters alike. An easy way to bundle a rope is to first fold the rope in half. Coil the doubled rope, beginning with the free ends, wrap the loop end around the bundle, and tuck it in.

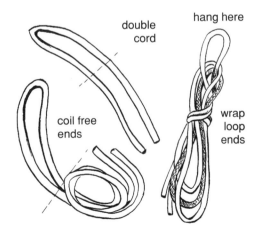

double cord

hang here

coil free ends

wrap loop ends

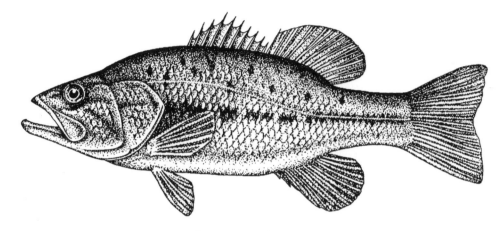

Largemouth Bass

COMMON NAMES

BASS, BIGMOUTH, BLACK BASS, BUCKETMOUTH,
GREEN BASS, LARGEMOUTH, LARGEMOUTH BLACK BASS, MOSSBACK

Largemouth Bass

When someone utters the word "bass," the first things that come to mind are probably lily pads, reeds, fallen trees, and stumps — all images that are usually associated with largemouth bass. Anglers can almost picture a bigmouth coming to the surface to inhale a surface lure.

When water temperatures reach 62 to 68 degrees Fahrenheit (16° to 20°C) largemouth start to spawn. Soon after spawning, they move to warm water bays, where they become the most sought-after shallow-water gamefish for sportfishermen. A slight change in temperature can determine whether the fish will feed aggressively or remain in a neutral frame of mind in heavy weed lines and other secluded cover.

Largemouths average 1 to 3 pounds (0.5 to 1.5 kg) in weight yet larger trophy fish are landed every year. Although there are many ways to catch largemouths using artificial lures, live-bait fishing is also a successful technique, because worms, frogs, and crayfish are part of the largemouth's normal diet. The following tips will ensure more "bassin'" fun on your next trip.

When fishing for largemouths, there are two ways to get one to hit:

- *Natural presentation* — Tempting the fish to take live bait or artificials that mimic natural prey.
- *Strike presentation* — Using the lively action of a lure to trigger a "strike by instinct."

Many anglers assume that dense weeds are comfortable holding areas for bass in the summer because they provide shade, which cools the water. Well, that's not exactly the way it works. The vegetation actually serves to collect heat in much the same way as a green-colored sheet would become hot if it were placed in the full glare of the sun. Because the weed covering heats the water around and under the weeds, the water temperatures in these areas can actually rise above those in weedless areas of equal depth. This is definitely the case in weedy spots without currents or wind action to flush out the heated water. So why do bass hang out in the weeds? The answer is simple. Weeds provide cover for all kinds of tasty tidbits that bass need to survive. This is why weeds should always be the number one location choice of the bass angler.

In sparse weed cover, adding a trailer hook to your spinnerbait or buzzbait can land fish that otherwise might not have been hooked. Always rig a trailer hook facing upwards. This will ensure that it's as weedless as possible.

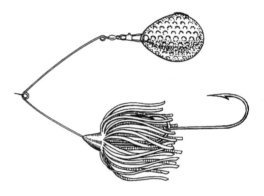

It's been proven in scientific experiments that largemouth bass possess color vision. Many anglers have sworn that certain colors are more productive than others. While each angler has his or her own favorite color, there are several common favorites, including purple, black, natural, and red. However, having several colors available in the tackle box can make the difference between fishing success and failure.

A word about weather. Largemouths are most predictable during stable weather.

During cold fronts, they feed heavily in advance of the front and then shut down until it has passed. Warm fronts stimulate feeding during the spring and fall but usually have the opposite effect in the summer. Thunder and lightning will stop bass from feeding, while storm run-off will attract bass searching for food that's been washed into the lake.

How many times have you passed up a spot or used an inappropriate bait because it was too much trouble to change the lure? If you have room in your boat, you can use an old trick of the pros. Rig up several rods, each with a lure chosen for a specific type of bass water. One rod might be rigged with a surface lure, another with a plastic worm for sluggish fish. A third rod might be a "flipping" rod, and so on. This will enable you to fish any type of bass "lie" effectively and quickly.

On calm days, in shallow water, make sure you cast *past* any likely looking structure that might hold bass. If your lure lands right on top of the structure, the fish might spook and not strike.

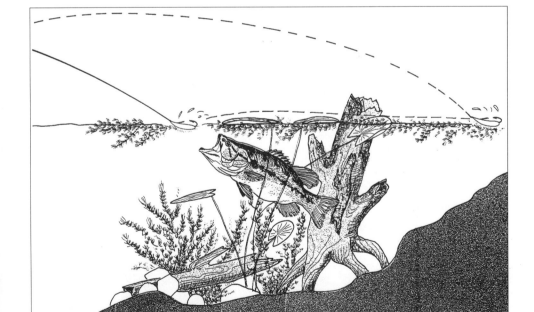

• Presentation is an important key to success. Try to "feather" your casts in shallow water so that your jig combos and soft plastic lures hit the target water with as little splash as possible.

• If you are using a weedless spoon and keep missing strikes, try adding a weedless trailer hook. Put a 1/0 trailer hook on the bend of the spoon then put a 4-inch (10-cm) Mister Twister on the main hook. Bury the tip of the trailer hook into the body of the twister. This adds action and deadly hooking potential to your spoon.

• If your fishing buddy hooks a bass in a certain spot, cast your lure to the same area. Several competing bass will often chase the same lure until one intercepts it. The "losers" will often strike a second offering if it's presented quickly.

• Although rattle lures do catch largemouths, this does not mean that sounds in general attract bass. Sounds to avoid include the splash of dropping anchors, banging noises in the boat from oars or tackle boxes, and gasoline motor noises. It's a good idea to place a piece of foam under your tackle box and to avoid oars and outboards in favor of electric motors. This is especially important when fishing shallow water.

• To make your Arbogast Hula Poppers and similar skirted lures look more lively, reverse the skirt so that it puffs out. This will give the lure a larger and more noticeable silhouette and will make the skirt pulsate better when the lure is retrieved.

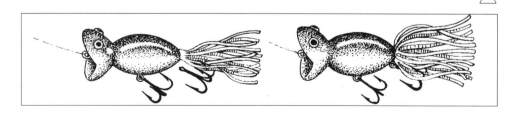

To increase the "weedlessness" of your lure, bend the blade arm of the spinnerbait until it almost touches the hook.

 When traveling from spot to spot, you can avoid line tangles, especially with your crankbaits, by putting one of the "save-a-pig," wrap-around jig holders on your lure.

 Structures — drop-offs, sunken logs, rock piles, and weed beds — are always a key to catching bass. But how do you choose from the bewildering variety of structures in a lake or river? Simply ask these questions: Does it provide cover from predators? Does it provide easy access to food? If the answer to both questions is "yes," give the spot a few casts.

 You can catch more bass if you understand a few basics about a fish's sense of smell. Gasoline, insect repellents, and other unnatural substances give off odors that repel bass. Certain odors, however, are thought to attract bass. Baitfish odors, for example, are marketed in great variety. The enticement of smell is also part of the reason that "sweeteners," such as minnows on the end of lures, work so well.

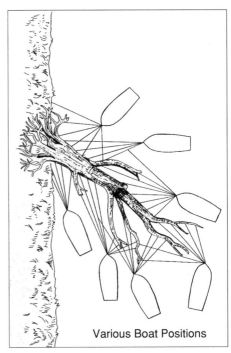

Various Boat Positions

 If you locate a wonderful piece of cover, such as a downed tree, make sure you cast several times to it. Slowly work your weedless lure all around the cover, because big fish sometimes take a while to be triggered into striking. Patience often pays off.

 Here's another tip to remember when you're fishing around a downed tree. Don't give up on it after you catch your first bass. Continue casting from the outer branches to the inner branches, and you might pull two or three bass from the same tree.

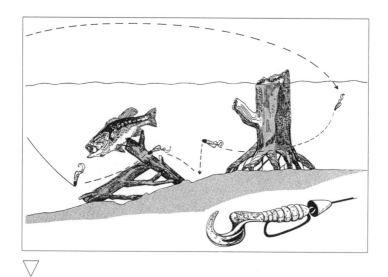

When the fish aren't biting, slow down your presentation. In many situations, the fish haven't moved away, but have simply shut down and are not feeding aggressively. A slow-moving twister tail jig or a worm "crawled" over a log or through the weeds can be tantalizing even to a lethargic fish. Remember, presentation is the key to success. When the bait settles to the bottom, pause, twitch the bait with your rod tip, and then pause several times during your retrieve.

If you like to use scented products, put your favorite plastic worms and twisters in a self-sealing plastic bag filled with a commercial scent for angling. Your baits won't need a squirt before casting.

Although largemouth bass are hardy fish, they can't simply be tossed back into the water. Take a moment to gently release them back to their watery home and you will help to ensure their survival.

Never assume that the only way to catch bass is with horizontal casts. Bass will hit lures that are presented vertically as well. Situations where "jigged" lures will work include the tops of dams, in a boat over a deep shoal, or from the edge of a drop-off such as a bluff.

Spinnerbaits are highly recommended for catching bass, but their effectiveness can be improved by choosing the right type of spinnerbait for your special fishing application.

➤ Do not purchase spinnerbaits
with weed-catching configura-
tions around the jig head. The
arm of the lure should run
straight out from the jig's head
rather than near its back and
there should not be any kind of
weed-catching gap.

➤ Here are a few tips for choosing
the right spinnerbait:
- *Spinnerbaits with round heads*
  create the best fluttering action
  and are good for sluggish fish
  that require a slow retrieve.
- *Spinnerbaits with pointed
  heads* are the most snag-proof
  and are particularly useful when
  working difficult weed beds.
- *Short-arm spinnerbaits* are
  designed for open water; they
  are not very weedless.

- *Long-arm spinnerbaits* are
  designed for weedy water; they
  are almost weedless.
- *Single-blade spinnerbaits* have
  to be retrieved quickly to keep
  the blades spinning; they are
  ideal when bass are very active.
- *Double-blade spinnerbaits* can
  be fished slowly; they are ideal
  when fish are not aggressive.

➤ The nice thing about spinner-
baiting for bass is that you can
interchange skirts, blades, and
trailers for different conditions,
thereby limiting your costs.
However, you should have at
least one short-arm and one
long-arm model so that you can
fish deep and shallow, and
weedy and open water.

➤ On lakes lined with summer
cottages and resorts, water skiing, jet skiing, pleasure boating,
and swimming force large-
mouths to adapt to nighttime
feeding.

➤ Use fast-running surface lures to
locate active largemouths in
shallow water.

➤ When fishing surface lures for
bass, always hesitate for a few
seconds before setting the
hook. Most beginners tend to
miss a fish because they set the
hook immediately.

On many lakes, wind and carp uproot vegetation, which is then blown to one area of the lake. This floating vegetation is often called "slop." Slop provides ideal surface cover for largemouths and should be fished at different times of the day.

When fishing slop, approach carefully and quietly. Drop your bait or lure in every opening that you go by. The largemouths in this type of cover are usually very aggressive and will hit immediately.

If you are having a slow day fishing for largemouth bass, try working a spinnerbait along any "bassy"-looking shoreline. By carefully casting to all structures and weeds along the shoreline, you should be able to prevent a "skunked" day on the water. This method often works for tournament anglers and should also work for you.

Because bass like protective cover, it's very important to fish docks, trees, stumps, and other objects that cast shadows over the water. Check out the sun's

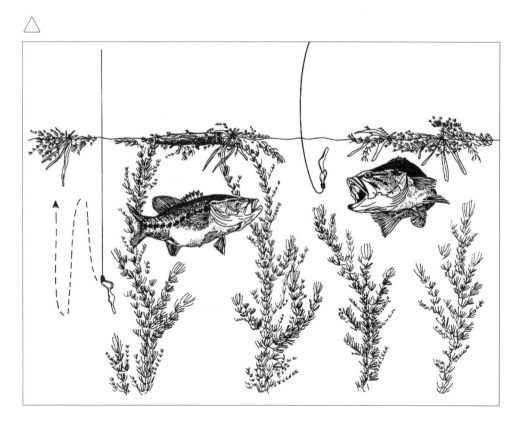

position throughout the day and fish the shady areas whenever possible. Because bass must make do with the structure or cover that is available to them, don't overlook unlikely-looking areas on lakes that lack cover.

The most productive cattails, reeds, and lily pads are those that are close to a drop-off or slightly deeper water. Although the depth change may be only 1 to 3 feet (30 to 150 cm), these areas can be topnotch for largemouth bass.

A **rubber frog** is an excellent artificial bait for catching largemouths in thick weeds. **Bill Plummer's Super Frog**, **Garcia**'s **Frog**, and **Mister Twister**'s **Hawg Frog** are some of the most productive. Fish these as slowly as possible right over thick cover.

One way to fish a rubber frog is to cast it on top of lily pads near the edge of an opening. Drag and hop the frog over the top of the vegetation. When you reach the opening, let the frog rest and wait for an explosive strike.

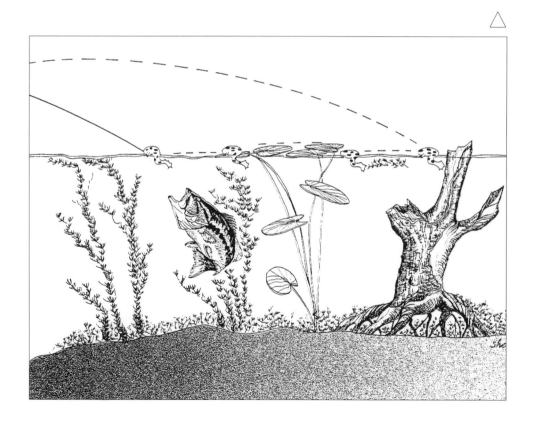

Adding a split shot to your spinnerbait's wire shaft can make it run deeper.

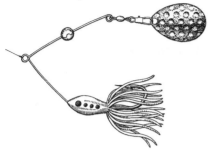

Surface fishing for bass at night isn't the only technique that works. Use spinnerbaits, plastic worms, and live bait in the same areas that you would fish noisy surface lures.

Full moonlight makes it easier to night fish; however, no moon at all provides the best overall largemouth bass fishing. Try using noisy poppers. A black surface lure is the best color choice, because fish can see black better than any other color against the silvery surface of the water.

The best time to begin night fishing is an hour or two before sunset. Get to know the area you will be fishing before the lights go out.

The best artificial baits for fishing slop are weedless spoons, plastic worms, and jigs.

One of the most novel ways to pursue bass is with the use of a special float tube. This device looks like an inner tube with a seat in the middle. It is used with diving flippers and lightweight neoprene waders, which keep the angler dry and warm. There are several advantages in using a float tube. First, it represents the ultimate in simplicity. There's no need to lug a big boat around with you, and you aren't dependent on a fishing partner to help load the cartopper. Second, it's perhaps the quietest method of stalking bass. A float tuber makes little noise and creates little shadow.

Many tournament fishermen have won tournaments by fishing docks and boathouses. Try casting along the sides of these structures using dark-colored jigs, grubs, and worms.

On large rivers, such as the St. Lawrence River, look for largemouths in protected bays and in adjoining streams and creeks that lack current.

Shallow-water largemouths are turned off by strong winds. If the winds are strong enough, they will leave shallow-water areas and go to the closest deep water.

One of the best bass lures is the plastic worm, hooked Texas-style (weedless). Purple and black are the best colors to use under most conditions.

Largemouths are most active in protected shallow-water areas of 68 to 78 degrees Fahrenheit (20˚ to 25˚C).

When largemouths refuse to hit your plug on a slow retrieve, try the opposite. Retrieve your lure as soon as it hits the water. Try to make a lot of noise. Those lazy bass might eventually decide to strike out of sheer irritability.

One way to correct short hits by bass is to add a "stinger" hook rigged in a regular or weedless style.

If you remove a largemouth from a particular spot, go back and try it again a few days later. As long as the spot provides cover and food, other bass will move in.

Any bass angler will agree that top-water lure fishing is one of the most exciting techniques there is. Noisy surface plugs, such as the well-known jitter-bug, can draw largemouths out of the tightest cover. Make sure you pause at least two seconds before setting the hook. The best times to use this technique are early morning or late evening, preferably over calm waters.

Largemouth bass often go for surface lures throughout the day. Try working a weedless lure, such as the Johnson's Silver Minnow or Breck's Timber Doodle rigged with a strip of pork rind or a twister, on top of lily pads. This combination usually triggers the big bass to hit.

If you are fishing the edges of weedy areas using live bait or artificial lures and you can't catch any fish, try using a weedless lure and cast into the weeds. At times, largemouths will sit in the thickest cover.

Largemouths, unlike smallmouths, don't like moving water. They prefer quiet back bays and channels.

You can make a strong, lightweight push pole for boating in shallow waters from 1¼-inch (3-cm) PVC pipe. Close the pipe with caps at both ends and you have a push pole for less than $10.

When bass are finicky about their food, try using a plastic worm fished across underwater points of land, near stumps, trees, and other thick cover. Bass can pick up the movement of these slinky baits even on the darkest night.

Bass often hear their prey before they see it. Their lateral line serves as a sonar and is effective up to distances of 20 to 30 feet (6 to 9 m). In deeper or murky water, rattling crankbaits and spinnerbaits work well.

When using a Texas-rigged plastic worm, wedge the worm

sinker in place by inserting the tip of a toothpick between the line and the sinker. This will keep your sinker close to the worm at all times, allowing a better drop and a more natural presentation.

- In many weed beds, large-mouths are buried deep within the weeds. Small spinner blades do not produce enough vibrations to draw these big bruisers out of their cover. In these conditions, change to a bigger, willowleaf type of blade on your spinnerbait.

- If you plan to fish seriously for largemouth bass, consider purchasing a medium-action baitcasting outfit. Baitcasters are usually stiffer than other rod types and can "horse" bass out of the heaviest cover. A baitcasting reel holds plenty of heavier line and will also enable you to make much more accurate casts.

- Shorter casts give you better line control and, therefore, better hook sets.

- Although fishing is usually not too productive during sudden weather changes, big bass can always be found in tight cover, especially under heavy weed mats and undercut banks.

- When fishing large weedy areas for bass, look for key ambush points that largemouths use when feeding:
  - Open pockets in a blanket of lily pads.
  - Long finger-like points of either lily pads or thick slop.
  - Channels or cuts between floating mats of weeds.
  - Weedy points jutting from straight weedy shorelines.

- Help enhance the scent of your pork rinds by soaking the pieces in solutions of anise oil or fish scents, such as Dr. Juice or Berkley Strike.

- Thunderstorms with a lot of lightning can spook bass. When fishing after an electrical storm, use a lighter line and a smaller lure. Make your casts past the target areas to keep the recently spooked bass from spooking again.

- After a thunderstorm, fish driftwood or log jams packed at the ends of some bays. These areas can hold schools of bass.

- If one of your favorite plastic worms gets ripped, just fuse the damaged part with a match flame. Give it a few minutes to cool before using it on another largemouth.

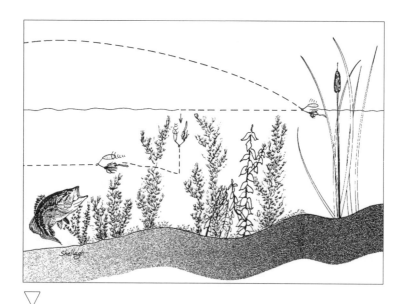

- When lures fished close to the surface draw "follows" but not strikes, let the lure drop. Most fish can't resist a falling bait.

- Largemouths are attracted to many types of vegetation that stick out of the water. Look for reeds, cattails, sawgrass, and wild rice.

- Old boathouses are prime "lunker" areas. Try casting your lure right inside and be ready.

- Natural baits are very effective. How can a largemouth refuse a helpless frog, minnow, or leech? Use a light split shot on the line so that the bait can move freely and look as natural as possible.

- When navigating in shallow water, it's important to travel as quietly as possible. If you make noise, the fish won't move far but you can spook them out of casting range or drive them into thick cover where you won't be able to follow them.

- If you are fishing a clear lake for largemouths, look for muddy creeks or areas that have an algae bloom. Bass sometimes congregate in these "stained" water areas.

- In lakes that contain both largemouths and northern pike, the largemouths are usually forced to live closer to the shorelines. The deeper weed lines hold mainly pike.

- Pattern fishing for largemouths can be very successful. If you are catching bass in a certain area or type of weed, look for similar areas in other parts of the lake. They should all hold bass. Look for successful formulas that can be applied to other lakes. That's the basic idea behind pattern fishing.

- Beaver dams are good areas for largemouths. Even after the beavers have moved to other areas, the remaining dam structures attract fish year after year.

- Cast parallel to shorelines with heavy cover. By keeping your lure parallel to the cover, it remains exposed to the bass for a longer time.

- The best lures for largemouths include flashy crankbaits, spinnerbaits, and surface lures.

- Sometimes you just need that little extra something to trigger largemouths to hit. Try using some pork rind as a trailer for your spinnerbait or even a different colored twister.

- Bass aren't bothered by strong sunlight in shallow water. Fish for them throughout the day with natural and brightly colored lures.

- Fishing for largemouths in boat channels in front of cottages can be very productive. Use plastic worms and work them slowly, close to the edge of the shoreline.

- In lakes that lack vegetation, look for largemouths along the shorelines or in slightly deeper underwater structures, such as rock piles and shoals.

- If your favorite "bassin'" shorelines are without fish, move out to the deeper waters near weed lines. These are nearly always productive.

- On windy days, always fish the lee or calm side of points, weed beds, and islands for largemouth bass.

- Largemouths love to feed on frogs. Leopard frogs are the most productive. In shallow water, fish the frogs on the surface. In deeper water, use a sliding live bait rig.

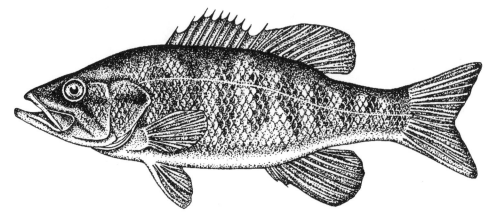

Smallmouth Bass

C O M M O N N A M E S

BLACK BASS, BRONZEBACK, BROWN BASS, GREEN BASS,
SMALLIE, SMALLMOUTH BLACK BASS, WHITE OR MOUNTAIN TROUT

Smallmouth Bass

The smallmouth bass is often said to be the wildest, strongest fighting fish in warm water. No fish can match the aerial acrobatic display of a battling smallmouth. It's common to see a fighting smallmouth somersaulting into the air and the fish flying one way and the lure the other.

The smallmouth bass is closely related to the largemouth, yet the species differ in many ways. One is appearance. The best way to tell the difference between the two bass is to look at the dorsal fins. The smallmouth's dorsal fin is one fin, whereas the largemouth's is divided into a front dorsal and a rear dorsal. Appropriately called the bronzeback, the smallmouth has copper, dark brown, or olive-green sides with darker vertical bars.

Unlike largemouths, smallmouth bass prefer cooler, clearer water containing rocks, drop-offs, and shoals. Smallies can reach weights in excess of 10 pounds (4.5 kg), but 1- to 2-pound (0.5- to 1-kg) fish are the norm.

Most largemouth fishing methods work for these fish, although they are usually caught in slightly deeper water than largemouths. Since smallmouths are fairly aggressive fish, they will strike crankbaits and other deep-diving plugs, which are very popular for deeper water smallmouth. One thing is for sure, pound for pound, bronzebacks will give you all the fight that you're looking for.

The following tips will help you locate smallmouths seasonally:

- *Early in the season* — Smallmouths are often in deep water that is close to shore and adjacent to spawning grounds.
- *Summer* — Smallmouths are found all over the lake in deep and shallow water along weed edges and shorelines.
- *Fall* — Smallmouths move to deeper water structure from 10 to 30 feet (3 to 9 m) in depth, closer to the main lake basin.

To catch huge smallmouths, try a brown flipping jig with a brown or orange pork rind trailer. This crayfish imitation is deadly for catching trophies even under the toughest conditions.

One of the most productive new lures on the market is the Gitzit. These tube jigs produce a slow, tantalizing spiral as they sink to the bottom. The erratic action can drive many lethargic smallmouths wild.

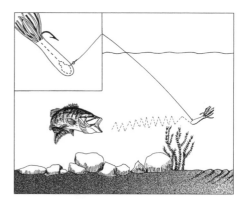

To prevent smallmouths from jumping and spitting your hook, stick your rod tip into the water as you fight the fish. This helps keep the fish down, resulting in greater landing success.

Many northern lakes contain only scattered vegetation. Trolling the shorelines with small Rapalas is probably the most effective method to locate smallies. Pick an irregular shoreline and troll in about 10 to 15 feet (3 to 4.5 m) of water. When you hook a fish, go back and see if there is something special about the spot by casting there again.

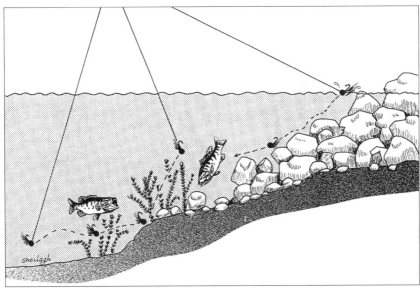

Here's a tip on how to adjust your smallmouth fishing to match the water clarity. In clear water, choose 4- to 6-pound test line. Keep your lure size small, choose natural patterns, and keep noise-making characteristics to a minimum. Use long casts and consider the use of live bait to fool wary smallmouths. In colored water, use the opposite strategies. Lines should be between 8- and 12-pound test, while lures should be large, noisy, and brightly colored. Casts should be shorter.

Smallmouths enjoy feeding on crustaceans. For this reason, smaller baits usually work best, especially jigs.

Smallies like weeds growing close to rough, rocky bottoms. To find these productive weed lines, follow any rock pile or bar that leaves a shoreline or island. The weed beds at the end of the rocks could be "honey holes."

In addition to trolling, still fishing for smallmouths can be productive. Anchor your boat close to a structure, such as gravel, rock, or sandbars, in 10 to 20 feet (3 to 6 m) of water.

Even in the summer months, smallmouths can be located in shallow, rocky shoals in the early-morning and late-evening hours.

By locating bottom structure in deep water, you can find schools of smallmouths that are just waiting to be fed. Try vertically jigging with spoons or jigs; you may hook one fish after another.

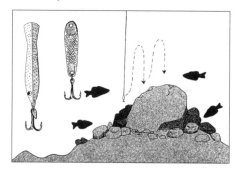

Bridge pilings and abutments are rarely fished, but there are always smallmouths in these areas throughout the season. Try casting crankbaits and jigs for some great smallmouths.

When fishing for smallmouths, be sure not to overlook man-made structures, such as culverts, sunken boats, or even boat docks. If it looks as though it could hold a fish or two, it probably does.

Many anglers assume that small-mouths will venture into shallow water only during the spawning season, fall feeding sprees, or at night. This is not always true. Some smallmouths will venture into water ranging from 1 to 2 feet (30 to 60 cm) in depth.

Never overlook spots with one or two large boulders in the water; smallmouths love to sit in the shade of rocks. At times these spots produce lunkers.

- In midsummer, smallmouths are often found in very deep water — 25 to 30 feet (7.5 to 9 m). One of the best ways to reach these fish is to rig a deep-trolling keel sinker ahead of a minnow bait. With this rig you can lower a top-producing lure down to these fish.

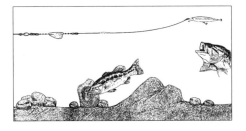

- Use the following baits depending upon the season:
  - *Early summer* — Use natural running balsa wood crankbaits without sound chambers. Shad Raps, the Rebel Fast Trac series, and Rapala Fat Raps are good choices. Fish these lures slowly, retrieving constantly.
  - *Midsummer* — Use a variety of crankbaits in larger sizes, in bright colors, and with sound chambers.
  - *Fall* — As the water temperature falls, use natural running baits again in imitative finishes, such as perch or crayfish. Vary the speed of the retrieve when cranking.

- When working shallow water with jigs, try dragging the jig and then bouncing it along the bottom by lifting your rod tip repeatedly. A different presentation just may help you box a few more fish.

- When fishing with jigs, use the lightest line possible. Most of the jig's action comes from the movement of your rod tip. A light line allows the jig to drop more naturally and produces a better action.

- For jig fishing, try to balance the line weight and the weight of the jig to the particular technique that you will be using. Different line and jig weights are used for drift fishing over rocky shoals, still fishing along weed lines, and casting in a productive stream.

- Smallmouths are schooling fish. It's common to stumble on a school and catch your limit very quickly.

- Some fishermen believe that bright sunny days mean poor fishing; however, smallmouths sometimes sun themselves in water that is less than a foot (30 cm) in depth. Under these conditions, use a small floating Rapala or other minnow-type lure that does not dive deep.

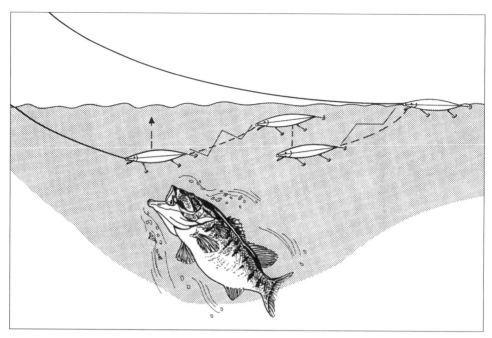

At times all anglers encounter fish that just seem to be off their feed. When this happens, you have to pull a few tricks out of your pocket in order to tempt "lockjawed" fish into hitting your offering. One of the most popular tricks is "twitching." Stick baits, such as the floating Rapala or Bomber Long A, are perfect for this tactic. Simply cast one of these lures out, let it sit for a moment, twitch it so it swims erratically for a couple of feet, then let it sit again. Repeat this maneuver as you reel your lure back to the boat. You will notice that it looks like a helpless, injured minnow struggling near the surface — a perfect target for a hungry smallmouth.

Many people don't realize how much fun it is to catch smallmouth bass at night. Heddon Tiny Torpedos, Hula Poppers, Dying Flutters, and small fly poppers are all good night producers.

Trolling at night with shallow-running Rapalas and surface lures works well for smallmouth bass.

Smallmouths move into shallow water at night, near underwater structure, and also over fairly flat sandy bottoms. Beach areas that are devoid of fish in the daytime can come alive after dark.

During the summer months, smallmouths are attracted to long points protruding far from shore. In the fall, they move to short, rounded points near the shoreline that have good rock structure or a combination of rocks and weeds.

Bouncing a crankbait along the bottom of a rocky shoal while reeling it in will often trigger a smallmouth to hit. The noise together with the stirred-up bottom usually does the trick.

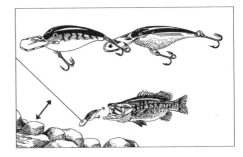

Other hot spots for smallmouths are rock piles and slides that have tumbled into the water along a regular shoreline. Smallmouths are drawn to these areas because they harbor crayfish and baitfish.

- Deep-diving wobbling lures are among the top producers for smallmouth bass all season long.

- Smallmouth bass are very territorial; a group of bass will occupy the same area year after year.

- On many lakes, the best way to catch smallmouths is by using minnows, frogs, crayfish, leeches, and worms. Try still fishing or drifting along shorelines, deep- and shallow-water structures, and weed beds and weed lines.

- Look for smallmouths near rocky shoals, drop-offs, and stony points. They may also be found where a rocky bottom meets the lake's weed lines.

- There's no question that crayfish are among the best baits for these fish. Unfortunately, most fishermen hook them through the tail, which usually results in missed strikes. Anglers should use a long shanked hook and fasten it to the crayfish with a rubber band. The hook's point should be near the crayfish's head. With this method, your bait will remain more active and your hook sets will be more productive.

- Over 50 percent of a smallmouth's diet is crayfish. Soft-shelled crayfish are favored over all else.

- If you snap off the claws of crayfish, they won't be able to grab weeds and will be less likely to crawl under rocks where the fish can't see them.

- Many anglers become perfectionists when it comes to lure action. Whether you're a pro or not, if your "bassin'" lure doesn't operate the way you think it should, do some fine-tuning. Try bending the tie-on-eye a little at a time until your fine-tuning catches fish.

- Smallmouths can easily be caught using fly-fishing techniques. Use streamers, wet flies, and surface poppers. There is nothing more exciting than setting the hook into a smallmouth that has broken water to take a surface fly.

Windy weather usually turns smallmouths on. Fish the shallow sides of shoals, drop-offs, and other structure. Smallmouth bass are drawn to these areas where the water is turbulent to feed on baitfish, crustaceans, and aquatic insects.

Trophy smallmouths can be caught in early summer when they are still spawning. Just cast jigs or crankbaits near their spawning bed, watch the fish attack, set the hook, and hold on!

Look for steep rocky banks with one or more fallen trees in the water. These areas will hold small schools of smallies all season long.

One of the best baits for drift fishing for smallies is the small worm harness and worm combination. Williams Fir Fly spinners and Hildenbrant spinners work well.

You can make any crankbait run deeper by adding a worm weight or split shot to the line just ahead of the lure.

River fishing for smallmouths below dams can be very rewarding. Smallmouths use currents to their advantage. They find ambush points and let their prey come right to them as they lie in wait downstream. Lures or baits approaching these waiting bass from behind rarely catch fish; they should move downstream toward the fish.

River tackle for smallmouths should consist of a spinning rod measuring anywhere from 6 to 7 feet (about 2 m) in length and a matching reel spooled with 4- to 10-pound test line. Small jigs and lures along with worms, minnows, crayfish, and leeches are the top producers.

Crankbaits are very effective for river fishing. The fast presentation lets you cover a lot of water quickly. Cranking is also a big fish tactic and often produces larger fish than jigs or even live bait.

Many of the streams and rivers that draw steelhead and salmon in the spring and fall harbor schools of smallmouths during the summer months. Take an ultralight outfit loaded with 4-pound test line and a handful of jigs and grubs and head to a small stream near you. The larger pools will always hold some smallmouths.

"River slipping" is an excellent boat-control technique that produces smallies. You can jig, cast plugs, or troll live bait very effectively using this method. Just face your bow into the current and keep your motor running in gear. The trick is to adjust your throttle so that

you're drifting downstream a little more slowly than the current.

 The best live-bait rigs for river fishing are the three-way drop sinker and Gapen Baitwalkers. Normal sliding rigs get caught up instantly in rivers with a fast-moving current and large rocks.

 Smallmouth bass aren't usually found deeper than 30 feet (9 m). One reason for this is the absence of crayfish past this depth. However, smallmouths in some lakes have to follow baitfish schools into deeper water in order to find food.

 When using frogs as bait, use small frogs such as spring peepers and immature leopard frogs. Fish them below the surface in deep water using a sliding sinker rig and on the surface in shallow water.

 When fishing lakes with channel markers, try live-bait fishing right by the marker buoys. Smallmouths will cruise up and down these deeper channels in search of food.

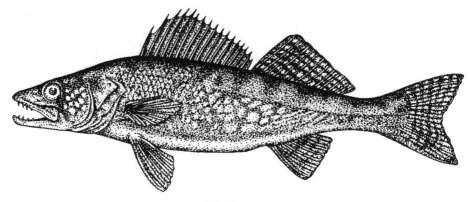

Walleye

COMMON NAMES

DORE, PICKEREL, PIKE-PERCH,
WALL-EYED PICKEREL, WALL-EYED PIKE, YELLOW PICKEREL

Walleye

One of the most sought-after gamefish in North America is the walleye. Most anglers will agree that this fish can't be beat for the wonderful texture and light flavor of its meat.

Even though this fish has been called a pickerel, the proper name is walleye. The term refers to the fish's glassy eyes, which are uniquely adapted for night vision. These exceptionally large eyes help the walleye find prey after dark and in the gloom of deep water.

The walleye is a spiny-rayed fish that is related to the yellow perch. As the largest member of the perch family, the walleye can reach a weight of more than 25 pounds (11 kg). The average walleye weighs about 3 pounds (1.5 kg). This fish prefers cooler water at temperatures of 50 to 70 degrees Fahrenheit (10° to 21°C) and is sensitive to bright sunlight. The most productive fishing times are therefore the low-light hours of the day. Night fishing is by far the most productive time.

Walleyes are piscivorous, meaning they feed mostly on other fish. Most of the time these delectable fish are caught by still fishing, drifting with minnows, or trolling.

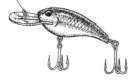

◄ Walleyes love currents and fast-water areas below dams. In these situations, extra split shot clamped onto your line ahead of your spinner, spoon, or crankbait will help it run deeper to reach the fish.

◄ If you are fishing new waters for walleyes, try these spots:
• Weed beds in the middle of the lake.
• Points along the shoreline.
• Bays along the shoreline.
• Structures, such as islands, bars, and deep holes.

◄ Here are some tips to predict where walleyes can be found during their seasonal migrations:
• *Spring* — Fish shallow-water areas. Rocky shorelines, shallow weed beds, creek and river mouths, and fast-water areas will hold walleyes immediately after spawning.
• *Summer* — Walleyes are found in deep-water structures, deep weed beds, and weed lines. Although some walleyes are found in shallow water during the day, most travel along shorelines at night. Fast-water

areas aren't as productive through the summer and draw mostly smaller fish.
• *Fall* — Walleyes are again drawn to shallower water and especially fast-water areas. The deeper water still holds some walleyes, but the best fishing is found around shorelines, islands, and shallower-water structures in depths from 6 to 15 feet (1.8 to 4.5 m).

◄ When you use jigs for walleyes, never exert a lot of pressure when playing the fish. Their teeth may be small, but they can still sever your line.

◄ On very windy days, lake populations of walleyes move into shallower water. Here they feed near shoals and rocky reefs where wave action stirs the water up and dissipates sunlight.

Few people fish with frogs for walleyes, but in late fall these fish feed heavily on frogs. Next fall go to your favorite walleye spots and try fishing frogs on or just below the surface.

In winter, to increase the distance over which your bait will attract walleyes under the ice, just attach a spoon (with the treble hooks removed) to your line. Then attach a leader about 6 to 10 inches (15 to 25 cm) in length to the split ring that held the hooks. Jig your bait up and down. The spoon will draw walleyes to the bait.

To locate shallow-water walleyes at night, listen for the slurping sound that the fish make when they're feeding on the surface.

During late fall, walleyes venture into extremely shallow water at night. They roam in schools in search of frogs and other amphibians that are forced out of the marshes because of ice-up. It's at this time that walleyes can be caught on surface lures in water 6 inches to 3 feet (15 to 90 cm) in depth.

- If you're looking for areas to fish late fall walleyes at night and in shallow water, try creek mouths, boat channels, and cattail shorelines.

- The best walleye baits for shallow-water surface fishing are twitching lures such as the No. 11 Rapala or the Rebel wobbling minnow.

- You can locate walleyes all summer long by using a flasher or graph depth-finder to locate structures in deep water. Vertical jig these areas with spoons, jigs, and live bait. You may stumble upon large schools of walleyes that few anglers have ever fished.

- The countdown method of fishing is great for walleyes. Just cast your lure out, count to four or so, then start retrieving. If, after a while, you don't get a strike, change your count until you hit the magic number.

- When Rapalas, Rebels, and other wobbling lures won't produce, switch to a spinner or worm harness and worm. Heavier spinning rigs such as Erie Dearies work well for both trolling and drifting. They can produce fish when nothing else will.

- Worms are an ideal bait for catching walleyes in rocky areas. Injecting air into the worm will ensure that it remains active for a longer time. Tackle stores sell plastic syringes known as worm blowers. Make sure the air is injected into the digestive tract, which runs through the center of the worm.

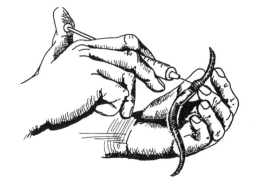

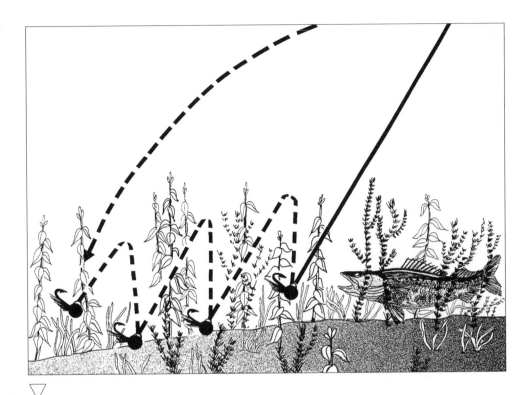

If you're jigging near heavy weeds and find yourself constantly struggling with weeds on your jig, try snapping your jig off the bottom. This will help you rip through the vegetation and, at the same time, your jig will drop in front of fish in a more natural way.

When using a jig for walleyes, retrieve the jig after it touches bottom by reeling in a little slack line while raising and lowering your rod tip. Repeat this lift-drop-lift-drop retrieve. A slow presentation is generally best. This technique can also be used in deep water where the jig does not touch the bottom.

Anglers who use jigs to catch walleyes often experience line twist. A quick and easy way to eliminate this is to tie on a small swivel 8 inches (20 cm) or so from the jig.

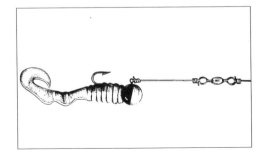

- Trying to decide what jig to use for walleyes is sometimes a problem. If the current is fast, choose a heavy rather than light jig. A heavyweight line also requires a heavier jig.

- Walleyes can be caught around sunken islands in the early morning and late evening, but during the day they disappear from these locations. This is the time to fish the open waters just off usually productive shorelines.

- In the spring, walleyes can be located in fast-moving waters such as waterfalls, dams, river mouths, and inlets.

- When using a minnow as bait, try snipping the tip off its tail. Because it will have difficulty staying upright in the water, it will move about more, attracting walleyes.

- Dragging live minnows, worms, and spinners along or just off the bottom works best at this time. If you use jigs, drag them along or just off the bottom as well, but use a slow presentation.

- Fathead minnows are an effective bait for walleyes; for some unexplained reason, the female minnows catch more of them. The females are usually more silvery and lack the bumps on the head that the males have. Shiners get the nod as the best second choice.

- During the summer months, walleyes can be found in deep water off shoals and along weed

lines. Most serious walleye hunters go after these fish at night when their nocturnal feeding habits bring them into the shallows.

◄ Whether fishing from shore or in a boat, remember that walleyes travel in schools. When you land one, work the area thoroughly; you should land a few more fish.

◄ A very slow presentation is preferred for walleyes, no matter the season.

◄ The best type of rod for catching walleyes is a medium- or light-to-medium-action spinning rod in the 7-foot (2-m) length range.

◄ One bait that's lethal for walleyes, and is sometimes overlooked, is the leech. Leeches work especially well in rocky, clear lakes and in fast water below dams. Drift the leeches right on the bottom or use a floating jig to suspend them.

◄ Because their eyes are very sensitive to light, drop-offs are one of the best places to look for walleyes.

◄ When fishing for walleyes on the bottom, a sliding sinker works well. Thread a ¼- to ½-ounce (7- to 14-g) egg or bullet sinker on your line, leaving about a 16-inch (40-cm) lead. Pinch a split shot on the line to prevent the sinker from falling down to the hook, then add your hook to the end. When the fish starts to take the line, it won't feel any weight, because the line travels freely through the sinker.

◄ Most people assume that walleyes are always on the bottom of a lake. This is not always the case. In most northern lakes during the summer months, walleyes suspend themselves above and below the thermocline — the layer that separates the warmer, oxygen-rich zone from the colder, oxygen-poor zone. They will migrate at these levels, following schools of herring all summer long. Deep-diving crankbaits trolled 50 to 200 feet (15 to 60 m) behind the boat work best.

◄ If you want more control of your bait while trolling, use the backtrolling method. Backtrolling is simply trolling with the motor in reverse. You'll be able to move more slowly and control your lure and boat speed better.

◄ If the walleyes tend to suspend at various depths in the lake you are fishing, invest some money in a manual downrigger. You can fish two rods from one rigger and lower or raise your bait to any desired depth.

◄ When trolling for suspended walleyes, you can use leadcore line, steel line, Pink Ladies, Dipsy Divers, and downriggers to help deliver your lures to the proper depths.

◄ If you are fishing for suspended walleyes and trolling isn't producing, try vertical jigging with heavy spoons 3/8 to 1 ounce (11 to 28 g) in size. At times, this is the most productive method.

◄ On heavily fished lakes, walleyes can become used to constant trolling pressure. Try using planer boards with Rapalas and worm harnesses in the areas that everyone is fishing. You may be surprised by the results.

◄ Many walleye fishermen don't realize that they can troll successfully with jigs. Trolling at slow speeds gives you total jig control, and you can cover a large area of water very effectively.

◄ If you are trying to bounce the lure off the bottom while trolling for walleyes and find that you are constantly getting caught up, use a Gapen Baitwalker in a ¼- to 1-ounce (7- to 28-g) size. Add a leader 12 to 24 inches (30 to 60 cm) in length and use floating, wobbling lures for better results.

◄ Walleyes prefer rocky or gravel bottoms. This type of bottom enables the fish to find food easily.

Many anglers have had great success with jig/minnow combinations. Keep the presentation as slow as possible while bouncing them along the bottom.

Walleyes have a delicate strike. Try holding the line in your hand just above the reel. This will allow you to feel the bite almost immediately so that you can set the hook quickly.

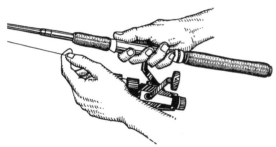

Walleyes in deep water aren't affected as much by surface changes in temperature, weather, and light as those in shallow water. If you are shallow-water fishing and not producing fish, go to those spots where you have caught fish in deeper water.

If you are fishing in shallow lakes, don't overlook stumps or lily pads. At times these spots will harbor walleyes as well as bass and muskies.

One of the best techniques for catching walleyes is drift fishing. Find some structure, such as a weed line or shoreline, and try letting the wind do the work. Drift with live bait or slow-moving lures. On very windy days, walleyes hold themselves still in certain areas to receive windblown tidbits of food, and the best way to find these fish is by letting the wind take you to them.

When drift fishing for walleyes, it's important to keep your rod tip down and slightly to one side, so that you can set the hook when you feel a tap. If you miss a strike, put the rod tip down again and stop your retrieve; the feeding walleyes may strike again.

If you are trolling and pick up one walleye, mark the spot. Blue Fox manufactures two great marker buoys; one is designed to be seen in fairly calm water from a short distance away, while the other is designed to be seen in rough water from a long distance away.

If you go to your favorite river to fish for walleyes and they aren't there during the day, try the same spot at night. Walleyes are known to move into the shallows at night to feed.

fishing at night. Pick a pier, dock, or bridge and cast in a fan pattern. The odds are you will catch walleyes randomly all night long. Walleyes will migrate quite far at night in search of food.

◄ When you are fishing fast water for walleyes, cast your jig up into the current. In addition to giving you more jig control, you will be bouncing the jigs right in front of the fish.

◄ If you are planning to night fish for walleye, make sure you take the following essential items along with the rest of your equipment: hand lantern, bug spray, anchor rope, life jackets, and proper boat lighting.

◄ When night fishing, instead of a bright flashlight, try using a black light with fluorescent line that can be seen up to 75 feet (23 m). Using this type of high-visibility line will enable you to see the strike before you feel it. Fish aren't spooked by the fluo-rescent line because the black light lights up the line for only the top several inches of the water's surface.

◄ Shoreline fishermen can also enjoy some successful walleye

◄ Walleyes are known as short-striking fish. They tap and nip at all kinds of bait. Try attaching a trailer hook to the end of your lure or bait and your success rate should go up.

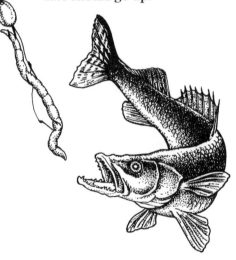

◄ When casting wooden plugs, such as Rapalas, in fast water, always start by casting at 45 degrees across the river and

allowing the lure to work as it is pulled down by the current. Then retrieve it against the current, pausing every 5 seconds or so. Most walleyes will hit on the pause.

◄ No matter what the season, walleyes can almost always be found near the lake bottom.

◄ Water temperature is the key factor to keep in mind when fishing for spring walleyes. If snow and cold temperatures keep the water temperature chilly, the spawning instincts of these fish are delayed until conditions are right.

◄ When jigging for walleyes with rubber, marabou, or bucktail jigs, tip the jigs with a minnow or a piece of worm. Once the walleyes get close enough to the lure, they will be tricked into striking.

◄ When you bag a walleye, pay close attention to where it hit, what type of current your lure was in, and the speed of your retrieve. By duplicating the original presentation, you should be able to land more walleyes.

◄ If someone says "jig and pig," you normally think of bass, especially largemouth. Believe it or not, these rigs are deadly on walleyes. Just attach a twin tail or pork leech on your favorite jig and spinner and see for yourself.

◄ When fishing with worms along the bottom, add a piece of Styrofoam in front of the hook to keep the worm off the bottom, or use a floating or neutral buoyancy jig. Either method will help you avoid getting caught up on the bottom and will produce more fish.

◄ Fish water that is 2 to 10 feet (60 cm to 3 m) in depth at night or in the early morning or late evening. During bright sunlight, fish the adjacent deeper water of 10 to 20 feet (3 to 6 m).

◄ Many walleye anglers use different colored twisters. They work all season long at all depths. Yellow, white, black, and pearl are the most popular colors.

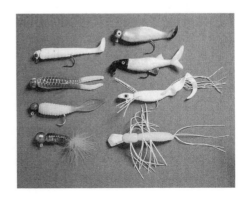

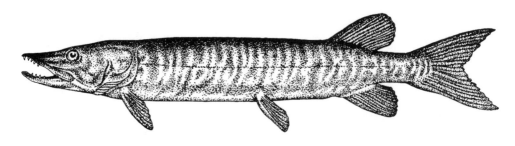

Muskellunge

COMMON MUSKELLUNGE NAMES

LUNGE, MASKINONGE, MUSKY, WISCONSIN MUSKELLUNGE

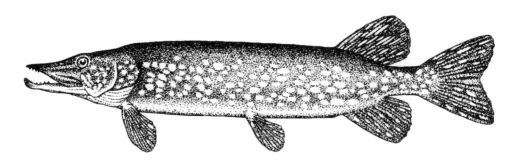

Pike

COMMON PIKE NAMES

GRASS PIKE, GREAT NORTHERN PICKEREL, GREAT NORTHERN PIKE,
JACK, JACKFISH, NORTHERN PIKE, PICKEREL, SNAKE

Muskellunge and Pike

Without a doubt, the muskellunge is the most prized of freshwater gamefish. Many versatile anglers have never hooked one. On the other hand, they've probably had many follows and didn't even know it. The sly musky will routinely follow a lure right to the boat, before turning with a good-sized swirl and then slipping back into the depths.

This ferocious-looking gamefish is often confused with the northern pike, but they differ in a number of ways. In appearance, the musky lacks scales below the eyes on both cheeks; in comparison, the cheeks of the pike are fully scaled.

Muskies spawn about two weeks after northern pike. They migrate to open water or travel up small streams and creeks. They prefer slightly colder and deeper water than pike and are known as solitary fish that cover large areas in search of food.

The musky is a much stronger fighting fish than the pike. Once hooked, it may run for a great distance, often jumping high out of the water while trying to shake the hooks free. Known for its aggressive strikes and spectacular, aerial acrobatics, it can snap conventional monofilament lines with ease.

Although they can grow to more than 50 pounds (23 kg) in weight, the average musky caught is between 5 and 10 pounds (2 and 4.5 kg). However, muskies in the 40- to 50- pound (18- to 23-kg) range are caught annually in Ontario. The world record is just over 69 pounds (31 kg) landed by an angler trolling in the St. Lawrence River.

Pike are frowned upon by many anglers because they often catch smaller fish; however, most of these anglers have never known the thrill of catching a fish over 12 pounds (5.5 kg). Smaller fish may be easier to catch, but hook a lunker and you've got a battle on your hands.

These warm-water gamefish live in shallow-water bays and drop-offs close to dense vegetation. Their varied diet includes minnows, frogs, snakes, crayfish, and other pike. They specialize in ambush tactics and will wait along weed beds or other cover for passing prey.

They spawn earlier than muskies, as soon as the ice melts, and prefer quiet, weedy waters 2 to 10 feet (60 cm to 3 m) in depth. Trolling, live-bait fishing, and casting are among the most productive methods for catching northerns.

- Fishing in the late fall for pike and muskies will definitely produce larger fish. These fish feed very heavily in preparation for winter.

- When trying to remove a lure from a pike or musky without pliers, always jam the mouth of the fish open with a large lure or even a stick, then proceed to remove your lure. This precaution may save your hands from cuts and scrapes.

- Since these particular fish have bony mouths, you may find that single-hooked lures work better. Generally speaking, it's easier to sink a single hook past the barb than a three-hooked lure.

- Pike tend to hang inside weed beds, whereas muskies most often cruise the outside edges.

- When live-bait fishing for muskies or pike, always wait for these fish to swallow your bait before setting the hook. Muskies and pike will take quite a while to turn a baitfish around in their mouths before swallowing it.

- Leaders are a must when musky or pike fishing. These fish tend to roll on the line when they are being fought. Use an extra long leader for the best results. If the leader isn't long enough, the line may be cut on the fish's gill rakers or fins.

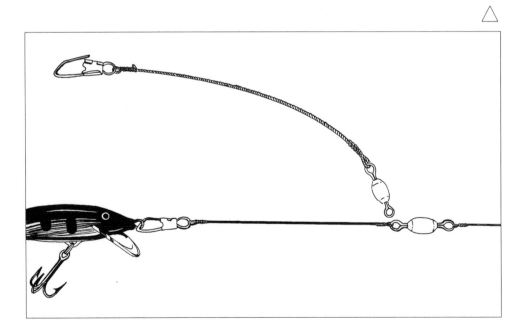

It seems a shame to see a good pair of pliers become sticky and unusable. After your fishing trip, place them in the front pocket of a pair of old jeans and run them through the washing machine. When the cycle is finished, your pliers will look like new. All you have to do is dry them and keep them oiled.

Big flashy spinners are readily taken by both muskies and northerns throughout North America. Cast or troll them near structure, shorelines, or weed beds.

An easy method for storing long wire leaders is to coil them together and then use a garbage bag tie to hold them in place.

If a musky or pike follows your lure to the boat, don't slow down your retrieve. Instead, reel faster to change the action of your lure. It just may trigger a big one to bite.

Mud, sand, and gravel flats located at river and creek mouths are ideal areas to look for muskies and pike.

When you locate small fish, such as perch, sunfish, and rock bass, you should also find pike and muskies looking for these same fish, their favorite forage.

More and more anglers are releasing trophy muskies and pike. Remember, the less you handle your catch the better. Since unhooking the lure is sometimes a difficult task, take hold of the fish by the head with your thumb and forefinger just behind the eyes. The other fingers should be pressed firmly against the skull bone. Remove the hook and place the fish in the water. Grasp your catch by the tail and hold it in place until it has enough strength to swim away on its own. If you intend to keep a pike, respect its sharp teeth and use a gaff.

If you're using premium monofilament line, make sure you use at least 25- to 30-pound test for big pike or muskies. You may want to try Dacron line if your hook sets are poor. Dacron has less stretch than monofilament.

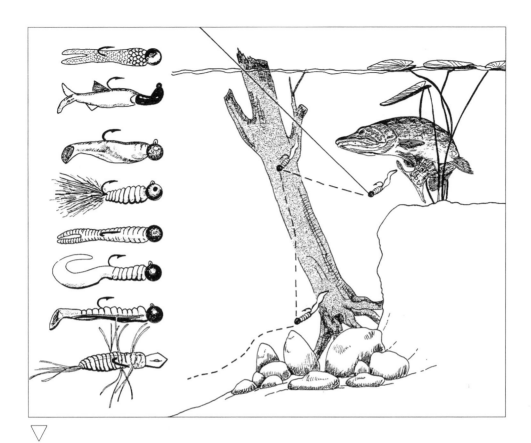

● Big fish sometimes go after lures that you would think are too small to appeal to them. Try using ⅜-ounce (11-g) twisters or Vibrotail jigs. You'll be surprised at how many 10- to 15-pound (4.5- to 6.5-kg) fish you'll catch.

● Trophy northerns and muskies can be found suspended in water depths of 15 to 40 feet (4.5 to 12 m) close to major structures, weed beds, and shorelines.

● Motor noise from your outboard may actually attract northern pike and muskies. Try some speed trolling, trailing about 25 to 40 feet (7.5 to 12 m) of line directly behind the boat. The prop wash and water agitation seem to stimulate the curiosity of these monster fish. After coming in close to the boat, they often strike a lure.

● Jerk baits, such as the Suick, are floating lures that do not possess their own action. The angler's rod has to provide the action for the lure. The Suick utilizes a rear metal fin and downcurved head to drive it underwater when it is jerked. Use a pumping motion, pulling the lure in and reeling in slack line, and then repeat the process.

◀ A Styrofoam cooler or pail is used by many musky anglers to store large musky and pike plugs. Just remove the lid, drape your plug inside, and pierce the last treble on the top inner edge.

◀ Some anglers who have many strikes but have difficulty hooking fish choose plastic musky and pike plugs over wood. Pike and muskies can imbed their teeth into wooden plugs, and when the angler tries to set the hook, nothing happens. A plastic plug slides between a fish's teeth until the hooks penetrate the jaw.

◀ Large suckers, 8 to 14 inches (20 to 35 cm) in length, make ideal baitfish for muskies and pike.

◀ In lakes with a lot of daytime boat traffic, muskies seem to become very lure-shy. In such areas, it's best to troll or cast at night. Large black plugs, moving just below the water's surface, work best.

◀ Muskies are not the least bit shy about feeding on the surface for small mammals, frogs, or waterfowl. You can take advantage of this by casting large Arbogast Jitterbugs or noisy bucktail "buzzbaits" near weed beds or stumps.

◀ Here's a trolling tip for catching king-sized muskies. Speed up your boat to about twice the speed you'd normally use for other species.

◀ The best musky spots in most lakes are along weed lines adjacent to deep water or near lake inlets, stumps, or log areas. Any points extending out into the lake are also worth a try.

Different types of wooden plugs jerked through the water close to the surface are great musky and pike baits all season long.

Because muskies are usually solitary and territorial in their habits, a large area must be covered in order to locate them.

When you've hooked and played out a good-sized musky and have it at your mercy right beside the boat, do yourself one favor — watch out. Muskies are notorious for producing one last thrashing run right beside the boat, often snapping the angler's line. Loosen your drag when a musky seems exhausted. If it does struggle at the last minute, the drag mechanism will simply release line and no harm will be done.

Muskies stay close to their home grounds, which contain weed beds, drop-offs, and even rock bars.

Keep in mind that most provinces and states have a minimum size limit for muskies. In Ontario, the minimum size limit is 36 or 40 inches (90 or 100 cm) in length, depending on the area.

- Whenever you hook a musky, try to land it as soon as possible if you intend to release it. Muskies, when running and jumping, experience a lactic acid build-up in their bodies. After they are released, this acid build-up can paralyze and eventually kill them.

- On many northern lakes, vegetation is sparse. On these lakes, troll the shorelines with Rapalas, Rebels, and other large musky plugs. Also cast to any points, deep bays, or islands.

- Lymphosarcoma is a cancer found in muskies and pike throughout their range. If you catch a musky or pike with one or more open sores on its skin, keep it and report your catch to the nearest Ministry of Natural Resources or Department of Fisheries and Oceans office. Not much is known about this disease, so authorities recommend not eating fish suffering from it.

- In shallow-water areas, you may see a musky lurking along a weed line. Don't assume that a fish that you can see won't hit your lure. Keep casting near it. Sometimes muskies will hit out of sheer aggressiveness.

- The chief food for muskies is other fish. Don't be afraid that the lure you are using is too large — the larger the better.

The muskellunge prefers slightly colder water than the pike and should, therefore, be fished in open waters of a lake rather than in the weedy bays.

Muskies like a faster-moving lure than northern pike. When trolling for muskies, increase your speed near deep weed lines.

The fall months have always been exceptional times for musky fishing. You should keep an eye on your lure during every cast and retrieve. If you think you see a follow, don't stop your lure; speed it up a bit and when it gets to the boat, maintain a figure 8 pattern. It just may entice a monster to hit at the last moment.

In clear water, large muskies tend to go into the deeper depths of the lake. No lure seems to be too big for these deep-dwelling trophy muskies.

Pike are known to hide in some of the weediest spots imaginable. You can use weedless spoons to fish these areas, but they have the disadvantage of having poor hooking power, particularly when the pike's bony mouth is taken into account. In very weedy areas, Heddon's Dying Flutters and other bass surface lures that don't pick up subsurface weeds can be very effective.

To find productive fishing areas for northern pike on hot summer days, look for large river mouths and cold-water springs in lakes. During the winter, holes in the ice caused by springs will give you clues about where to look during the summer.

Any of the larger spoons will produce pike anywhere, anytime. Silver and red-and-white patterns are the most popular.

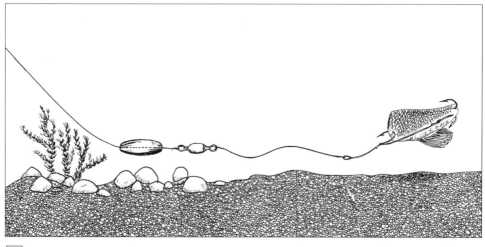

- In the early spring, dead baits can actually outproduce live baits because pike scavenge the baitfish that have died during a long, hard winter.

- Most seasoned pike anglers use black wire leaders. In a pinch, you can make your own pike leaders by purchasing heavy monofilament line (17- to 30-pound test) and some snap swivels and barrel swivels. Homemade leaders are cheaper and you can make any length you want.

- Don't be surprised while fishing tight cover for bass if you hook a big pike. Like bass, pike also like protection from the sun.

- Early morning is the best time to catch pike.

- If you want a lure that covers a lot of water fast, use a white or chartreuse spinnerbait. If pike are feeding, they'll go after this bait if your presentation is right.

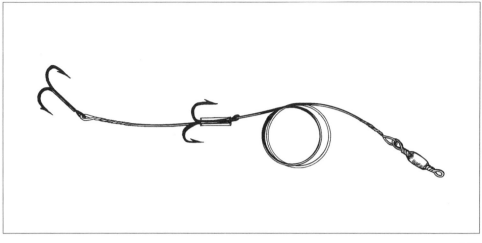

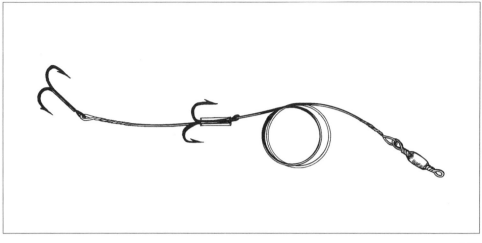 Northern pike are delicious, but should be skinned and have their "Y" bones removed before you eat them.

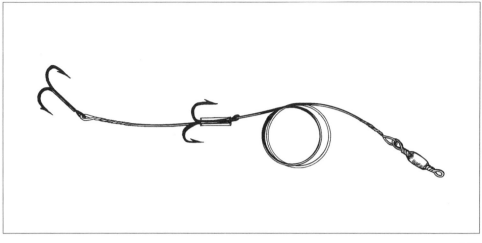 Pike are usually found in greater numbers than muskies in shallow water. Numerous pike will move in and occupy a weed bed, whereas only one or two muskies will be found in the same type of bed.

 Pike usually slash at the bait to kill it before turning it in their mouths and swallowing. One of the problems of bait fishing for pike is knowing when the bait is firmly in the pike's mouth so the hook can be set. This is largely solved with quick strike rigs, which have two hooks, one on each end of the bait. The hook can be set immediately with this type of bait.

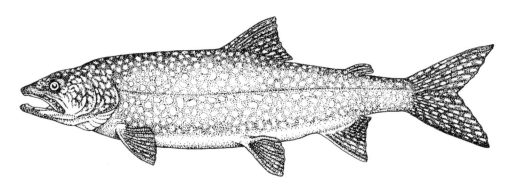

Lake Trout

COMMON SPECIES

....

BROOK (SPECKLED), BROWN, LAKE, RAINBOW, STEELHEAD

Trout

A great variety of freshwater species are available to the river, stream, and small lake angler. In this chapter we concentrate mainly on fish that are commonly called trout.

Probably the most majestic trout is the steelhead, the anadromous version of the rainbow trout. ("Anadromous" refers to fish that spawn in freshwater rivers and then move to the sea.) The fish is native to the west coast, but has been introduced to the Great Lakes. Steelhead spawn in the spring and fall. It's at these times that river anglers gather to hook these hard-fighting fish, which are capable of long runs and frantic jumps.

Catching these fish when they are spawning is a specialized task. They usually ignore normal food at this time. Spawn sacks, which are the size of a dime and consist of trout or salmon eggs tied in a fine netting, are the most popular stream bait. Spinners, plugs, and spoons also work well.

Native rainbows, browns, and brook trout are, unlike steelhead, much smaller and do not migrate back to the sea or a Great Lake after spawning. Typically, they feed on insects and small minnows. Anglers often pursue these feisty fish with a fly rod or light tackle, and with flies or small spinners and spoons that imitate the most popular forage available to the trout at the location the angler has chosen to wet a line.

- Don't use a steel leader when trout fishing. Trout may be able to see this type of leader; besides, you don't need one in any event, because most trout don't have teeth big enough to cut your line.

- Is there a good fish in the pool, or not? To find out, catch a grasshopper and remove one leg before tossing it upstream from the pool. If there's a feeding trout around, it will usually not pass up this free meal. Now's the time to give it your all with your favorite fly, bait, or lure.

- Here's a good way to catch natural bait for stream trout. Attach a square piece of screen or nylon mesh to two pieces of strapping. Hold this in the

Current

water and walk slowly upstream, moving stones and debris with your boots. You'll be surprised at the different types of bait that you capture in the screen. So will the stream trout.

- When bottom bouncing for stream trout or even salmon, there are several different egg-type presentations to choose from — a roe bag, yarn fly, skeined spawn, or even dyed sponge.

Quartering a plug or spinner across the current of a river allows the lure to arc right in front of waiting salmon or trout. This brings the lure into the fish's strike zone.

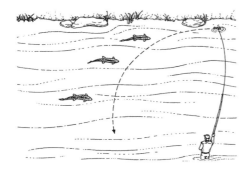

The key to covering fast sections of a stream is to make multiple casts, working from the closest to the farthest trout lies. Always cast the bait well ahead of the strike zone to create a natural drift.

For fast-water bait drifting, make sure your sinkers are spaced closely together and near the bait for tighter line control.

For slow-water bait drifting, make sure your sinkers are spaced apart and away from the bait to allow your drift to be as natural as possible.

One of the most difficult pools to fish are those overhung by alders or other vegetation.

Every time you attempt a cast from across the stream, you tend to snag up in the bushes. Try this. Use a small float, strip some line from the reel, and walk the float downstream past the bushes from that (the bushes') side of the stream. Step lightly and feed the line out with your hand. Remember to hold on to the line with your hand when you set the hook. As soon as possible, close the bail and feed the loose line out again as the hooked fish struggles against the line. It's a bit difficult, but it works!

If your line becomes badly twisted after using a spinner all day, simply tie on a spoon with a ball-bearing swivel and toss it around for a while. This will remove the worst of the line twist.

Spinners should be chosen according to water visibility. A silver No. 4 Mepps Aglia would be a good choice for a flooded river, while a black No. 1 or No. 2 Aglia would be perfect for clear waters.

If the water is low and clear, fish the pools and the middle of deep runs. Try changing to a float and single-egg technique and fish at various depths.

If the water is high and dirty, fish the upstream section (the head) and the downstream section (the tail) of pools first. Try drift fishing close to the bottom and covering as much water as possible with every drift.

At many times throughout the year, trout gorge themselves on freshly hatched insects. If you own a spinning rod and reel,

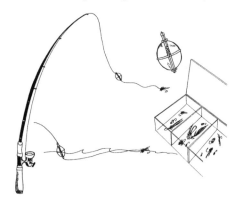

you can find some fine action. Attaching a plastic bubble approximately 3 feet (90 cm) ahead of a small fly will not only add extra casting weight but will also ensure that you don't spook the trout.

When using a float and roe-drifting technique, remember to match the float to the various conditions:
- *Low, clear water* — Use a very small float, such as a porcupine quill or a tapered English-style float. Use minimum shot

(4 to 8 BB shot is the recommended weight) and very small hooks. The light floats will move most naturally in slow water.
- *Faster water* — Use a larger float and weigh it down. A 3 to 5 0/7 shot is recommended. This will slow down your drift so that your bait is suspended in one spot for the longest possible period of time, while still looking natural.
- *Large rivers* — Use a float and heavier line. The recommended weight of shot to use is 3 to 5 0/3.

Early in the season, fish pools where the current is slow. These spots usually show up in stream bends right after fast, shallow rapids.

Small garden worms fished with small hooks and light line will draw strikes when nothing else works.

In clear water, use the smallest hooks possible (No. 10-18 trout hooks) and bury the hook in the bait you are using.

Always approach a potential holding spot for fish from downstream. The fish will be lying with their heads pointing upstream and will spook less readily.

It takes some practice to read moving water and to decide where the fish are. Try fishing near undercut banks, points, bridge abutments, fallen trees, and even large rocks.

You can increase your catch by learning to cross over the river and fish the opposite shore when the situation calls for it. Often one side is easier to fish or offers better cover that helps prevent you from spooking holding fish.

For something a little different, try casting your fly onto the bank and pulling it into the water. Throughout the day, trout spend time waiting under overhanging banks for insects to fall into the water.

Fish are often concentrated in fast pools. A better method than casting and retrieving is current drifting. Just attach a minnow-like lure to your line with a few split shots attached to the line about 2 feet (60 cm) in front of the lure. Cast near the top of the pool and let the fast water do the retrieving for you.

Small minnows are always deadly for trout early in the season. Hook the minnow lightly through the lip, lob it gently, and let it do its trick. When you feel something tug at the line, wait a moment and then set the hook.

A wide range of flies works well for trout, especially during the early morning and late evening. Just "match the hatch" — use flies that imitate the insects that are hatching on the stream that day.

Many trout anglers pass up the best spots in the stream because they're too hard to reach. By using a longer rod and a flipping technique, you will be able to reach these fish-holding spots.

Instead of attaching split shot sinkers to your fishing line, attach them to a piece of line as in the diagram. If your split shot becomes wedged between some boulders, a tug may strip your weights, but not the rest of your rig.

Try to use the lightest float you can when drift fishing. The resistance to being pulled under the water of the heavier floats will chase any potential takers away.

Most stream trout feed on all kinds of insects that fall into the water. They also love crayfish, frogs, worms, and minnows. All these work well as live bait.

Most trout like cooler water. Look for deep pools or springs entering a stream. These areas can hold large numbers of fish.

If you fish rivers and streams in cold temperatures, try wearing rubber gloves. Not only do they keep your hands warm, but you can also still bait your hooks and feel the hits.

Undercut sections of banks as well as fast water below a dam should provide plenty of action.

During the summer months when the water levels are down, you'll catch more trout if you use smaller lures.

When wading in a trout stream, try walking with the current and, at the same time, turning over small rocks and logs. Your actions will dislodge all kinds of food, which will be carried downstream to waiting fish. This prepares them to take your offering.

All trout species are very alert in their home waters. Try to use the lightest possible fishing line. You need every advantage you can get.

If the water is dirty from a heavy rain and the fish are "shooting" the rapids, switch to drift fishing the bottom. Set the hook at the slightest twitch or snap, since the fish may hit very lightly in these conditions.

When approaching a trout stream, always keep a low profile and, if possible, cast your bait before you get too close to the water's edge. Trout have very good vision and the refraction of light off the water gives them a "window" that allows them to see not only the surface but also the bank.

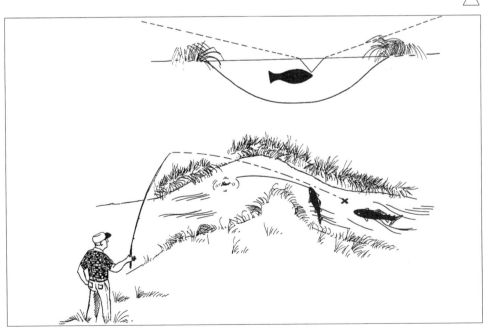

- If plugs don't produce, try an assortment of spinners. Vibrax, Olympic, Mepps, and Panther Martin spinners in silver, gold, and black are some of the most productive.

- When fishing with nymphs or grubs, try to make short casts. Your bait will stay on the hook longer and stay alive longer, too.

- When wading in fast and/or deep water, use a wading staff to help maintain your balance. Remember to move slowly and sideways to the current if you can. Here's where a fishing buddy can help. One person takes a few steps and finds some safe footing, then reaches out to the other person, who walks up to and past him by a few steps until he finds a secure place to stand. The maneuver is then repeated.

- Fish in the shallower waters of a river or stream when it is rising. Fish move toward the shallows to find food and escape fast currents.

STEELHEAD

- Steelhead run up rivers in the spring and fall. Although most steelhead spawn in the spring, there are also some fall-spawning steelhead populations.

- Choose the right colors for steelhead floats: chartreuse-tipped floats are most visible under low light conditions, while black floats with fluorescent orange tips are most visible in bright sunlight.

- Steelhead are well known for raising their heads up out of the water in a vigorous head shake that often results in thrown hooks or broken lines. To prevent this from happening, simply decrease the line tension by lowering the rod a bit. This will cause the fish to drop beneath the surface again. The rod tip can then be raised once more.

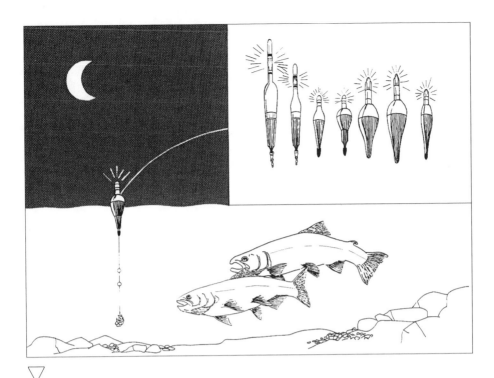

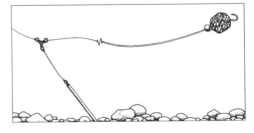

Pools with spooky steelhead can be fished successfully at night with the aid of a night float. Blue Fox makes a variety of lightweight floats, which are powered by a lithium battery. Fishing at night may be the only way to catch these fish, and the odds are good of catching some brown trout as well.

Spawning steelhead can become quite aggressive at times. The fly angler can capitalize on this by retrieving streamer flies through pools of medium depth. Steelies will also hit wet flies such as the Michigan Wiggler or the Stonefly Nymph. These are especially effective when they're drifted through riffles below a pencil float or a strike indicator.

If you like to drift fish large rivers from a boat for steelhead, use thin, pencil-shaped lead weights to take your bait down to the bottom. This type of rig is one of the most snag-proof bait rigs you can use.

◄ The best time to fish for steelhead is after two or three days of heavy rain. As the water starts to drop and clear, the steelhead stop running and hold in pools. This is when they are most active.

◄ A longer rod and light line are used to catch steelhead. Most steelhead rods are 9 ½ to 13 feet (2.8 to 4 m) in length and are

made of fiberglass, graphite, or boron materials. Line weight varies from 2- to 10-pound test depending on the water conditions. Lighter line is used in clear water with no snags, and heavier line is used in dirty water with snags.

◄ Dawn and dusk are prime times for steelhead. During rainy, overcast days, steelhead fishing is good all day long.

◄ Dams and other obstructions will stop and hold steelhead for weeks or months. Some steelhead will remain in the rivers most of the summer. These fish have surprised many trout anglers. "Hold-over" steelhead will feed actively and, if not spooked, will hit almost anything that comes near them.

◄ When steelhead are spawning, they dig a redd. These egg-filled nests appear as light patches of gravel between 1 and 3 feet (30 and 90 cm) in diameter. If you notice these areas, look for fish on the redds or just above and below. Spawning fish can be teased into striking.

◄ During the fall when salmon are spawning in the streams and rivers, try drift fishing immediately below these fish. The odds are there will be steelhead eating up eggs just below.

◄ Always wear highly polarized sunglasses when steelheading. They will help you to determine water depth as well as to spot fish.

When using a float for steelhead, you should always use a swivel below the float with a leader that is lighter than the main line attached to it. This will serve two purposes: (1) if you get caught up on the bottom, the lighter leader below the swivel will break and you will still have your float; and (2) if a fighting steelhead starts to roll on the line, which they often do, the line won't get twisted because of the swivel.

When fishing pools with many holding steelhead, use as small a hook as possible. This will decrease the chances of foul-hooking a fish (hooking a fish accidentally in the body) and will still give you good hook sets.

When fighting a leaping steelhead, dunking the rod into the water will create more drag and torque and will prevent the fish from jumping.

Two of the easiest ways to land an exhausted steelhead are to beach it or to tail it with a 100 percent wool glove. (Wool does not remove the protective slime from fish.) Normark's mesh fillet glove is also an excellent tool to use for tailing fish.

- When still fishing from shore for steelhead, use two Y-shaped sticks or metal rods to make a very efficient rod holder. It will keep your rod and reel off the ground, preventing them from being damaged by sand and dirt. Push the sticks into the ground until they are stable. Make your cast, then place the rod into the holder, leave the bail open, and place a small pebble over the line on the ground to keep it taut. When a fish hits, it will be able to take the line freely. Just set the hook and hold on.

- When trying to locate steelhead in a river or stream, it's very important to learn to read the surface of the water:
  - *Slick water* — This usually means an even, shallow bottom that holds fish only when the water is discolored or high.
  - *Rapids* — These mark the head of a run or pool and may indicate a sharp drop in depth. Rapids can hold steelhead at any time.
  - *Slow water below rapids* — This indicates a pool area. The water will be deeper here, and steelhead will hold in these areas when the water is clear and low.
  - *Tail ends of pools* — These are found where the deeper water turns to slick water. Steelhead spawn in these areas, which can be extremely productive in the spring.

SPAWN AS BAIT

- Salmon eggs, trout eggs, and worms are the most productive baits for drift fishing for steelhead in streams and rivers.

- Spring anglers sometimes catch ripe female trout but end up losing most of the eggs when carrying the fish. Always keep a sewing needle in your fishing vest and sew the vent closed with monofilament line to ensure that the eggs aren't lost. You can also squeeze the eggs into a plastic bag before transporting the fish.

- Use smaller spawn sacks in clear water and larger sacks in dirty water.

- Throwing a handful of fish eggs into a pool before drift fishing will increase the odds of hooking a steelhead.

- A piece of fluorescent orange or yellow yarn placed on the hook above a spawn sack can make the difference between getting strikes and not getting strikes in dirty water.

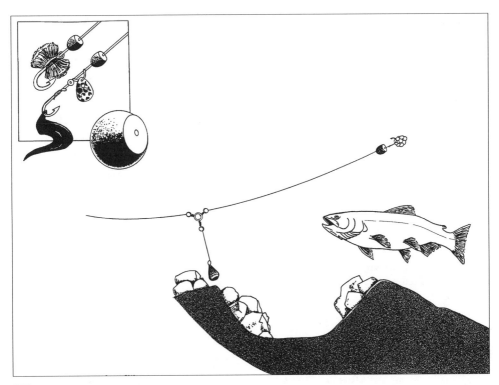

● Li'l Corkys and Blue Fox's new Dr. Juice Bait Float Juicers are small Styrofoam balls that look like salmon eggs. Place these on your line above the hook. As they slide back and forth, they attract fish and keep the spawn sack off the bottom.

● Ideal water visibility for steelhead fishing occurs when you can see a bait 6 inches to 1 1/2 feet (15 to 45 cm) below the surface. Test the water visibility as a rain-swollen river clears by dunking your roe bag into the water every now and then.

● Cheese rolled up in the shape of a fish egg and canned sweet corn are good replacements for trout and salmon eggs.

● Always remember to change your spawn bags every 15 minutes or so, especially in harbors and other still waters. After a while, spawn loses much of its scent and "milking" effect. ("Milking" refers to the dispersal in water of the internal material contained in an egg. The material often appears as a milky cloud surrounding the spawn bag.)

- Use naturally colored netting for spawn bags in clear water. Spawnee brand netting in yellow, white, orange, and pink works well.

- If you catch a female steelhead with fresh roe, the eggs will last for only a short period of time in the refrigerator before spoiling. There are several ways to preserve your eggs so that they will last for the fishing season:
  - *Freezing* — Trout and salmon eggs should be thoroughly washed in water, air-dried on newspaper for about 15 minutes, then placed in a glass or plastic container or a bag. Try to remove as much air as possible from the container or bag before placing it in the freezer.
  - *Salt treating* — Wash eggs and stir them in a brine solution made up of uniodized pickling salt and water. The more salt you use, the tougher the skin of the eggs will become. Let the eggs sit in the solution from two to fifteen days. Remove, air-dry, and store them in an airtight container in the refrigerator.
  - *Borax, boracic acid* — Eggs should be washed, air-dried, and sprinkled with either borax or boracic acid powder. Once they are completely covered, place in an airtight container

and refrigerate. If you choose, you can make a saturated solution with these chemicals and leave the eggs in a bath.

- Skeined trout eggs are eggs that are still attached together with membrane. Those treated with powdered borax turn a deep

orange and become a solid mass. When the skeins become firm, pieces can be torn off and placed directly on the hook. In clear water, nothing looks more natural than skeined eggs.

- Stockings and leotards are the most common materials with which to tie eggs. Cut the material into 2-by-2-inch (5- by-5-cm) squares, place three to six eggs in the center, then lift up the corners and form a sack. Twist the top, tie it off with thread, and trim with a pair of scissors.

- One of the best-kept secrets of avid steelhead anglers is the use of spawn sacks made of women's light nylon scarfs in bright colors. They are highly visible in dirty water.

When drift fishing fast-water areas, a small piece of sponge in the color and shape of a spawn bag, which has been dipped in scent or fish oil, can work better than real roe.

You can color trout and salmon eggs with food coloring to whatever shade you prefer, from gold to hot orange and pink.

To store treated eggs in the refrigerator, add a few drops of phenol to prevent mold for several months.

You can prepare single salmon eggs so that they can be fished on a hook without falling off by boiling or briefly frying them until they become firm. Single eggs together with light line can prove deadly in clear water.

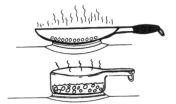

Nylon stocking pieces will hold your roe; however, if you substitute hot orange and pink nylon netting for the stocking material, you'll be amazed at how many more strikes you'll get. To a trout, color is very important.

Take your spawn-tying material when you go steelheading; after you catch a female trout, nothing beats tying fresh eggs and using them on the spot.

When fishing the bottom, use some Styrofoam in your roe bag to keep it suspended off the bottom. This technique works extremely well when steelhead congregate at river mouths and when they are holding in large pools.

If drifting eggs and worms don't produce fish, switch to casting plugs. Small Flatfish, Kwikfish, Fire Plugs, Tadpolys, and Hot

Shots work well. Black, silver, green, and orange are the more productive colors. Fish these with the current and against the current. Fish them shallow and deep and vary the retrieve. At times these plugs will out-fish drifting baits.

RAINBOW TROUT

angler doesn't even notice it's gone. A quill float or some other type of buoyant strike indicator will tell you when a fish has picked up the bait.

◄ Fish trout pools from the tail to the head (downstream to upstream). A fish caught downstream will not necessarily spook other rainbows holding near the top of the pool.

LAKE TROUT

◄ If a large rainbow trout runs under a log jam or similar obstruction while on your line, don't give up. Allow the line to go slack, and sometimes the fish will leave the area on its own. Another possibility is to ask your partner to create a disturbance on the other side of the obstruction to scare the fish into running upstream again. A last resort is to attempt to thread the rod itself under the log jam and continue the battle on the other side.

◄ Stream rainbows can sometimes take a bait so lightly that the

◄ The best way to fish a small lake for trout is by using a boat and casting toward the shore.

◄ During the spring when lakes are very cold, lake trout stay close to the surface, so trolling with a flat line (sometimes called a high line or surface line) can be very productive.

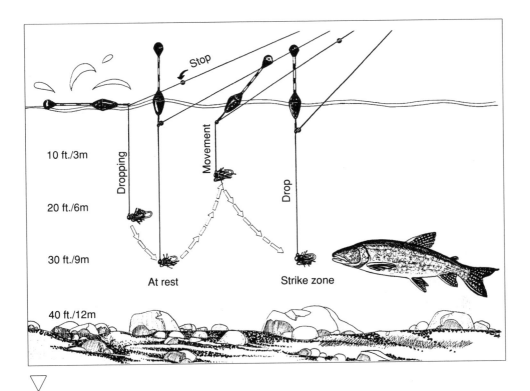

10 ft./3m

20 ft./6m

30 ft./9m

40 ft./12m

Dropping

Movement

Drop

At rest

Strike zone

Stop

Through the fishing season, lake trout are found only at particular depths. The best way to fish a specific depth is to use the float-jigging technique. The line, tipped with a jig, is allowed to run through the center of a slip bobber until it hits a bobber stop, which is attached to the line at exactly the needed depth. When the line is pulled up through the float, the jig dances under the water at precisely the right depth. At the moment a laker picks up the lure, the float dives, telling the angler exactly when to set the hook. This is one great rig!

When lake trout are found only at great depths, the best way to catch them is with a downrigger; however, a less expensive and less complicated device for reaching these fish is the Dipsy Diver. This device is attached to the trolling line and will move it away from the boat and down to a predetermined depth. Once a fish is hooked, the Dipsy Diver is tripped so that it does not offer much resistance in the water, enabling the angler to fully enjoy an unencumbered battle with the fish.

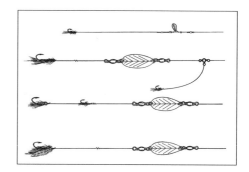

The "Christmas tree" or "gang troll" is one of the oldest and most popular lake trout lures. It consists of a number of spinning blades and spoons rigged closely together on a leader. To this gang troll is added a piece of monofilament with a bait rig. The many flashing spinners and spoons resemble a school of baitfish and attract lakers from afar. The bait rig actually hooks the attacking trout.

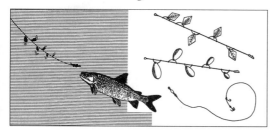

When trolling for lakers at depths of 40 to 60 feet (12 to 18 m), it's important to choose lure colors that will be visible to cruising fish. Fluorescent colors, such as orange, pink, and chartreuse, are visible at any depth. Natural colors, such as blue, green, and black, are also a good choice. A rule of thumb is to use the fluorescent colors on overcast days and the naturals on bright, clear days.

One of the most effective rigs for lake trout trolling is the spoon-fly combination. Simply remove the treble hook from a spoon and replace it with 12 inches (30 cm) of monofilament holding a flashy wet fly or streamer. The spoon attracts fish from great distances, while the fly draws the strike.

Jigging for lake trout with a bucktail jig and minnow or strip of fish can be very productive over the summer months. Look for drop-offs and other structures in water 50 to 300 feet (15 to 90 m) in depth and try drifting or vertical jigging.

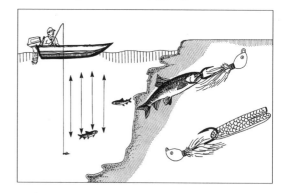

Silver Williams Whitefish and the standard Williams lures are top-choice spoons for lake trout angling. Canoe-type spoons are

the second most popular type
of laker lure.

- Lake trout feed mainly on herrings in deeper water. Shiny
spoons and plugs work well
fished with leadcore line, steel
line, or with downriggers.

- In small lakes, try locating a
beaver lodge. The branches
usually provide plenty of cover
for trout and their prey.

BROOK TROUT

- If brookies are constantly biting
off the lower half of your worm,
try using a "stinger." Just attach
a worm-sized length of 2-to 4-
pound test line to your hook
and tie on a second, preferably
smaller, hook. Thread the
worm over both hooks so that
one hook is near the top while
the second is near the bottom.
Now invite that short-striking
brookie to try again.

- Stream brook trout are wary, so
it's important to walk upstream
to all your favorite pools. Walk
quietly and try to present a low
profile, which is more difficult for
the fish to see. Some anglers even
resort to camouflage clothing.

BROWN TROUT

- If you've spotted an enormous
brown trout in a large pool and
can't get it to hit your lure or
bait, special tactics are called
for. Try hooking a 2- to 3-inch
(5- to 7-cm) creek chub lightly
through the skin behind the
dorsal fin, just to one side of the
backbone. Another bait worth
trying is a small frog hooked
through one leg. The secret to
success is timing. The best time
to fish these baits is at night. Be
patient and wait for the fish to
come to the bait. This technique is especially effective in
big, slow pools under bridges
or in large pools with deeply
undercut banks.

- Brown trout are the most difficult of the trout species to
catch. Fish for them at night or
when the water is discolored
after a rain.

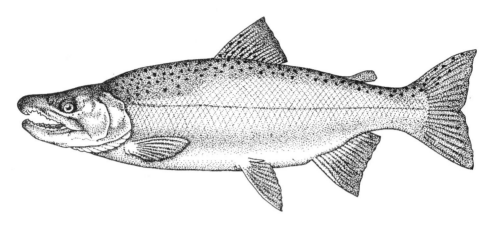

Coho Salmon

COMMON SALMON SPECIES

CHINOOK (KING), COHO

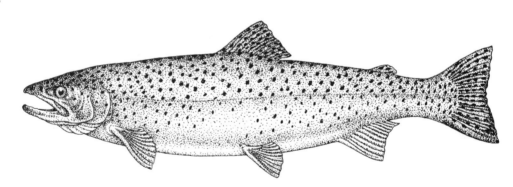

Steelhead Trout

COMMON TROUT SPECIES

BROWN, LAKE, RAINBOW, STEELHEAD

Great Lakes Fishing

With nine salmonoid species available, it's no wonder that many anglers enjoy fishing the Great Lakes, where fishing derbies promoting cash prizes of up to a million dollars have been held.

The variety of gamefish presents a true challenge for any angler. Those who want to catch salmon and trout consistently in the Great Lakes must be familiar with today's modern electronic techniques. Electronic depth-sounders and graph recorders indicate the water depth and type of bottom. They also show gamefish and baitfish, both individually and in schools, as well as bottom structures such as shoals and sandbars.

As inhabitants of cold water, salmonoids prey on alewives, smelts, herrings, and other small fish. Special fishing techniques are used to catch them, especially in the midsummer months when they are mostly found in a fluctuating temperature zone called the thermocline. Today's sportfishing marketplace offers nearly invisible fishing lines and lures that duplicate baitfish. Downrigging, a fishing method that uses a lead weight to take lures down to deep-swimming fish, is now a universal technique. Salmon that have weighed close to 50 pounds (23 kg) have been caught with downriggers, but the average runs from 10 to 20 pounds (4.5 to 9 kg). Fishermen also use spoons in a variety of colors to catch the many types of fish available throughout the Great Lakes.

A fishing diary is a helpful tool for Great Lakes anglers. Recording such facts as the date, time of day, water depth, lure depth, lure color, lure size, and lure speed on each fishing trip will help you become a more consistent angler. When the same conditions occur again, you'll know what worked in the past.

Wait for sporting goods stores to hold sales on lures. You may not find the right colored spoon, but with a little paint and prism tape, you can imitate your favorite lure at a fraction of the cost of a new one.

Compressed air has been used for years to clean cameras and lenses. A can of compressed air costs about $10 and is a great device for ridding your graph recorder and/or flasher of dust, dirt, and carbon.

In the spring, try using a flat-line (sometimes called a high-line or surface-line) technique and troll jointed Rapalas in chartreuse, blue, or fluorescent red close to shore.

Salmon and trout are excellent fighters and often end up wrapping themselves in the line and breaking it. When this happens, it's a good idea to troll back over the area. You never know, your fish might be disabled in the line and floating right on the surface.

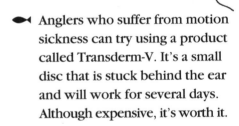

Anglers who suffer from motion sickness can try using a product called Transderm-V. It's a small disc that is stuck behind the ear and will work for several days. Although expensive, it's worth it.

In the Great Lakes, schools of salmon are often seen porpoising near stream mouths several weeks before they make their spawning runs. They are actively feeding and always on the move. However, because these fish seem to spook quite easily in shallow waters, instead of trolling through and around them, try casting to them with spoons, spinners, or plugs.

- Here's a good rule of thumb. The earlier or later in the day you fish from piers, the closer you should fish toward shore. As the sun rises and sets, salmon and trout move out into deeper waters. On overcast days, these fish also stay closer to shore for a longer period of time.

- When smoke rises straight up, expect no change in the weather.

- Spring and fall are the best times to fish from piers. In fact, as soon as the ice is out and the water warms up a little in the spring, you can get a jump on the boaters.

- Vary the depth of your lure as you retrieve it. This will help you locate salmon and trout in early spring when they gravitate toward shallower water and become accessible to shoreline and pier anglers.

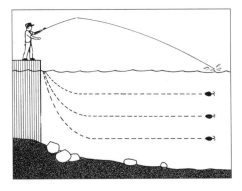

- Try replacing the treble hooks on some of your lures with single hooks. You'll find that you'll lose fewer fish using a single hook because it penetrates better than the treble hook. It also enables you to unhook your catch more easily so that you can release it without handling it too much.

- Hydrographic maps make it easier to locate long, sloping underwater points, submerged river channels, drop-offs, and shoals. In the spring, these areas generally hold large numbers of salmon and trout, because they feed on the baitfish that congregate in shallow waters to spawn.

- When fishing a large lake, especially Lake Ontario, remember to keep an eye on the weather. A wind change can result in very rough water. Make sure your boat is large enough to handle rough conditions or be prepared to head for shore.

- To keep your boat clean, purchase a large, high-quality cooler and mount it on your swim platform. Not only will you be able to keep your fish on ice, but you will also end up with more space and a cleaner cockpit.

- Sometimes a little extra flash on your spoons will trigger salmon to hit. Pick up some prism tape in a few different colors — chartreuse, blue, and green are favorites — and experiment.

- Rubber squids occasionally stick together when they are left to dry in a tackle box. Just drop them in a small plastic bag with a little talcum powder, shake, and they'll be ready for your next dodger-and-fly combo.

- When lifting a good-sized fish into your boat, raise the net on an angle to minimize the strain on the handle. Most Great Lakes anglers like long, extendable net handles for landing big bruisers.

- A high visibility marker is very useful when you're fishing the Great Lakes. You may want to mark the location of a group of salmon or baitfish and then swing around and troll back in your favorite pattern.

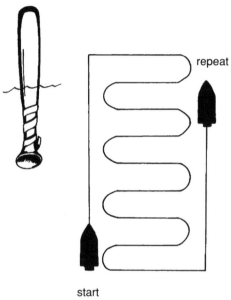

repeat

start

- Even in the hot summer months, early morning is a good time to look for cruising rainbows, browns, and chinook salmon. They come into the shallows at that time for baitfish and retreat to the deeper waters as the day goes on.

- Before you spend thousands of dollars on equipment for fishing the Great Lakes, you should go out on a fishing charter. Talk to the captain about his equipment and make sure that what you are thinking of buying is suitable.

◄ Thermoclines (temperature breaks in the water), muddy lines along river mouths, and debris and algae lines in deeper water often offer some heavy salmon and trout action. Baitfish are located in these spots and their predators are seldom far behind.

◄ Refrain from giving a fish away — it usually ends up in the garbage. If you're not sure of the catch limits in your area, return the fish to the water so that it can survive and reproduce.

◄ Spring fishing for salmon and trout is always fun. Why not experiment with different ways to entice these fish to hit? Try different trolling speeds, use zigzag or S-type turns, and fish in front of warm-water outflows.

◄ Many anglers try to run a variety of spoons and plugs at the same time as they search for feeding salmon and trout. However,

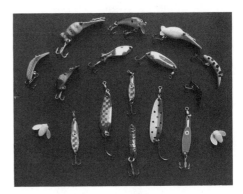

many of these lures are designed to achieve their maximum action at specific trolling speeds. For this reason, if you want to run a spoon and plug together, make sure they are "speed compatible."

◄ Both CB and VHF radios are much more than safety communication devices. You can also receive weather reports and valuable fishing advice, such as the best lure of the day to use, the best overall fishing depth, the best trolling speed, and the location of the hottest action on the lake.

◄ If you're unsure where to fish on open waters, look for other boats. When the fishing is productive, a pack of boats forms quickly. Be cautious,

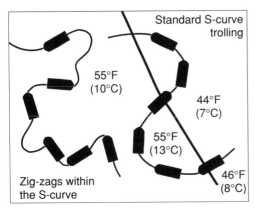

Standard S-curve trolling

55°F (10°C)

44°F (7°C)

55°F (13°C)

46°F (8°C)

Zig-zags within the S-curve

however, when using planer boards in such crowded conditions. A boat may cross your line or your line may become entangled with another line. Many big salmon are lost this way.

- To obtain a good hook set when you are downrigger fishing, tighten your reel so that your rod tip is bent downward as far as possible. By pulling the line toward the reel with one hand, you can reel up the slack quite easily with the other.

- When you run out of releases, an elastic band will work just as well. In fact, many fishermen prefer using elastics; they do less harm to your fishing line and are certainly much less expensive. Pull one end of the rubber band through the other onto your fishing line until it snubs tight, then attach it to a snap-swivel on your downrigger wire.

- If you are marking fish on your graph recorder and there are no takers at the particular depth you are fishing, stagger several downrigger lines at varying depths and lengths from your cannonball until you find the magic combination through trial and error.

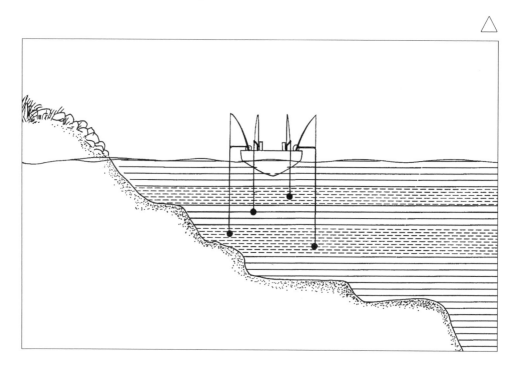

You can also use your downrigger in the spring while fishing shallow water. After running out a long lead of about 100 feet

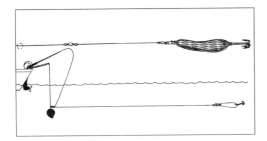

(30 m), attach your fishing line to the release on your downrigger. Lower the cannonball a foot or two (30 to 60 cm) into the water and tighten your rod into a heavy arc. Your rod is now ready for a good hook set and shallow-water action.

Downrigger cables and release clips can play havoc with your fishing line. Before each outing and throughout your fishing excursion, check for frayed, peeled, or nicked line. The damaged line should be removed and replaced.

Cannonballs and sinkers can be made quite easily from reclaimed shot, which you can purchase from your local rod and gun club. Small shot is probably the cheapest source of lead that you'll find, and takes less time to melt than block lead.

If you use crankbaits on your downriggers in early spring or late fall, remember that they will dive several feet (nearly a meter) deeper than the downrigger ball setting.

Try using a heavier cannonball (10 to 12 pounds/4.5 to 5.5 kg) when you are fishing deep or rough water. The few extra dollars spent on a larger cannonball is money well spent. Your downrigger cable will bounce less in rough water and will track closer to the boat, enabling you to pick up the cannonball on your graph recorder.

When a good-sized salmon hits, it's wise to pull in other lines to eliminate tangles at boatside. Cannonballs should also be reeled in so that they're out of the water. A wire cable can slice through a monofilament line, cutting your trophy loose.

If kinks develop in your downrigger wire, it may break, sending your releases, lures, and cannonball to the bottom. Why risk it? Snip the line and splice it back together with crimps or, if badly kinked, replace the entire wire line with a fresh roll.

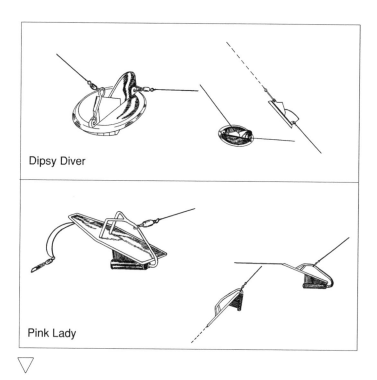

Dipsy Diver

Pink Lady

If you don't have a downrigger to get your lure down to the proper fishing depths, try using diving planers such as Pink Ladies or Dipsy Divers. The more line you let out, the deeper these devices will track. Many 20-pound (9-kg) plus salmon have been caught by these inexpensive devices.

Planer boards, also called trolling boards, give the Great Lakes fisherman five major advantages:
- A larger area of water can be covered.
- More lines can be run with fewer tangles.
- Lures remain away from the boat's path and stay in the fish's strike zone area.
- Lures can be placed in shallows, even to 3-foot (90-cm) depths, without worrying about hitting bottom with the prop.
- Lure speed can be changed with shorter turns.

Downriggers can be used with planer boards. Just turn your downrigger out 90 degrees to your transom, attach the planer board to your cable, and let it go out to a maximum of 50 feet (15 m). This simple technique can move your lure away from the boat. Be aware, however, that the cable could break under heavy stress. This technique should be avoided in rough water.

➤ A planer board release can be made quite easily with an alligator clip and a metal shower curtain bracket. Slip some thin rubber tubing over the tips of the alligator clip to help secure your fishing line. Secure the two by soldering.

➤ When using a planer board, make sure your outside line is the farthest one behind the boat and the shallowest. The lure running on the inside should have a shorter lead and run deeper. These tips will help prevent tangling when the fight is on.

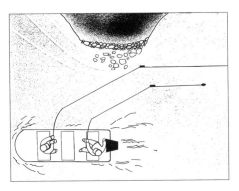

➤ When chinooks aren't hitting your offerings at the other end of the downrigger, try lengthening your lead. This is especially important if the salmon are, in fact, showing up on the sonar. A normal distance between cannonball and lure is about 15 to 20 feet (4.5 to 6 m). Try extending that distance to 40 to 60 feet (12 to 18 m) to pick up fish that are too "spooky" to hit normal presentations.

➤ One of the problems encountered in downrigger fishing for chinooks occurs because the current speeds near the water's surface can be different than those much deeper. A lure that runs perfectly on the surface may wobble too quickly if a fast subsurface current is moving in the opposite direction to the boat. A lure may also move too slowly if a fast surface current is moving in the same direction as the boat. The solution is simple. To minimize the effects of unpredictable subsurface currents, always use lures that provide a lively action over a wide range of speeds. The J-Plug is a good example.

●◄ One of the best ways to entice cohos when you are using multiple downriggers is to run an entire set of spoons. This imitates a school of baitfish. To really fool the fish, bend one of the lures so that its action is impaired slightly. This makes it resemble an injured baitfish and turns it into a target for marauding cohos.

●◄ Don't neglect the use of lures when fall-running chinooks enter the rivers. These fish, particularly the males, will angrily charge flashy spoons, spinners, and even large plugs, such as the J13 Rapala.

●◄ The principal food of most chinooks in the Great Lakes consists of alewives. These fish are different sizes at different times of the year. If possible, examine the stomach contents of a salmon to determine the size of the baitfish. By matching your spoons to the size of the alewives, you'll box more "kings."

●◄ Water stratifies into distinct temperature layers during the hot summer months. Knowing the preferred temperature zones of the species you want to catch can improve your odds. For example, chinooks, which are probably the most sought-after salmon species, are found between 49 and 52 degrees Fahrenheit (9° and 11°C).

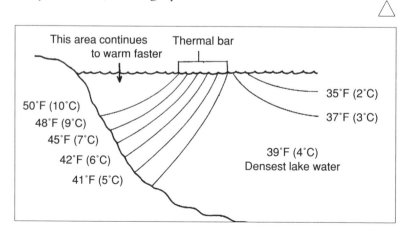

This area continues to warm faster

Thermal bar

50°F (10°C)
48°F (9°C)
45°F (7°C)
42°F (6°C)
41°F (5°C)

35°F (2°C)
37°F (3°C)

39°F (4°C)
Densest lake water

When fishing for chinooks near harbors, there are a few ways to increase your odds. Use spoons, because they cast farther with less effort than plugs or spinners. Always spread your casts out in a fan shape to cover more water. And hold your rod tip pointing at the direction of the cast and just above the water's surface so you'll be able to get a good hook set.

Chinook salmon, especially immature ones ("jacks"), are fond of eating one another's eggs. In the river, pairs of chinooks can often be spotted on a redd (nest). If there's a pool or run below a spawning pair, get your rod ready with a small spawn bag or even a single egg as bait. Any "egg eaters" at work in the area will be particularly vulnerable to this presentation.

When you're fighting a coho in a large lake, there's no need to hurry the fight or take any risks. As long as the fish is not threatening to spool off all of your line, it is unlikely that it will snag the line or create other problems. All you have to do is allow the fish to run and gently "pump" it back toward you when it slows down. By taking your time and repeating this sequence repeatedly, you will seldom lose a fish.

TROUT

Shallow-water brown trout in large lakes are often very wary of the troller's boat and lures. It is necessary to run extremely long leads of 100 yards (91 m) or more. An even better solution is to use a planer board, which presents the lure off to one side of the trolling boat.

Often an entire school of lake browns will come shoreward and roll about within casting distance, but they won't hit artificial lures. Lure anglers even snag these fish accidentally. To catch these fish, rig a spawn bag under a slender float or through a sliding sinker and float the bag just off the bottom. Again, patience is called for until the fish find the bait, but this technique really works.

If the trout are hitting roe bags, and you catch and keep a lake brown loaded with eggs, don't miss your chance to stand out from the rest of the pack. Take some of the eggs and tie them into a piece of sacking material. Browns seem to prefer fresh roe over cured or frozen eggs.

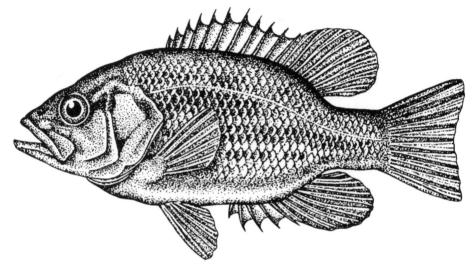

Rock Bass

C O M M O N   S P E C I E S
....

BLUEGILL, BULLHEADS, CRAPPIE, PERCH, PUMPKINSEED, ROCK BASS, WHITE BASS

Panfish

ne of the most enjoyable types of fishing for young and old alike is panfishing. Even experienced pros had to start somewhere and many of us, no matter how much we've fished, still enjoy the thrill of hooking a plump bluegill or a perky perch. Indeed, sampling the spring crappie run or the fantastic ice-out perch fishing is enough to get anyone's juices flowing before the more popular gamefish seasons open up. Light-tackle enthusiasts, including fly-fishing fanatics, are discovering the challenge of casting tiny flies for spunky panfish.

The species, lumped under the term "panfish," are found across North America, making them almost universally available to all anglers.

the minnow suspended near the fish, you can jig your bait right in front of its nose.

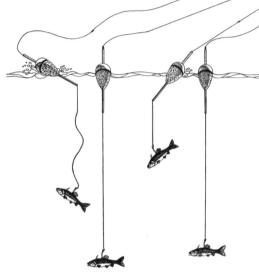

- Because panfish are readily available throughout most of North America, they are a great way to introduce the very young to the enjoyable sport of fishing. Don't keep children out too long on their first few outings, though, especially if the fish are biting. The repetition of catching fish after fish can become boring for them.

- Try fly fishing for panfish with a variety of attractor pattern dry flies, such as poppers and hoppers. Rather than imitating insects or baitfish, these flies attract fish with their bright colors.

- One of the best ways to catch panfish is by casting a minnow rigged under a slip bobber. Because the slip bobber keeps

- Use one or two split shots to weigh down your live bait when fishing for panfish. Bell sinkers and other commonly used weights are too heavy and make feeling the bite much more difficult.

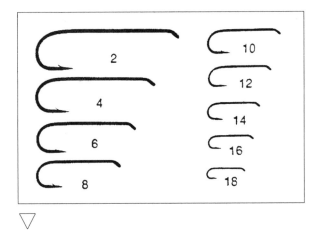

Don't use the hooks commonly sold in most stores for worm fishing with a bobber. They are often much too big for tiny bluegill or pumpkinseed mouths. The best hooks to use are small fly-tying hooks that have a long shank but a small hook gap. They are the perfect size for these fish to engulf and are easily removed from their mouths.

Although many anglers think of periodically checking their knots and line when fishing for large gamefish, it is equally important to check your line for nicks and abrasions with smaller fish. Nobody likes to lose a favorite crayfish jig to a small fish.

One of the best ways to attract panfish to come within easy fishing range is to "chum" the water with small bits of bread or cooked pasta (subject to local regulations). Break these up in small pieces and throw them out as far as you can. Panfish will find the free tidbits within a few minutes.

If you're live-bait fishing and run out of worms, simply look around for beetles, grasshoppers, or other insects. They are a good substitute for worms and keep the fish biting.

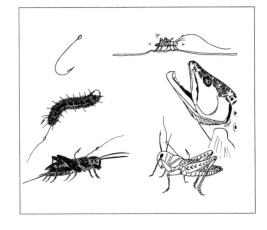

CRAPPIES

● Use extremely sharp, fine wire hooks when fishing for crappies. Their paper-thin mouths can easily tear if you put too much pressure on them when setting the hook.

● When you are fishing known crappie-holding water, be patient. Often the fish will move in suddenly, feed quickly, and then move out again. You have to stay and wait them out in order to get in on a fast-paced bonanza.

● If you live near good crappie lakes or ponds, check them every few days in the spring so that you don't miss the big early-season run. The run lasts only a few weeks in most places.

● Try to release most of the largest crappies that you catch so that they can go on to spawn superior offspring.

● The lightest jigs, in the 1/8 to 1/64 ounce (3.5 to 0.5 g) sizes, are the most productive jigs for catching crappies.

● A highly productive technique for locating and catching crappies all summer long is trolling slip bobber bait rigs. You can easily adjust the depth of your bait, and the bobber will signal a strike.

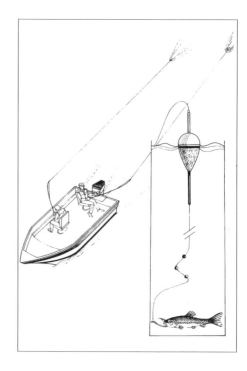

PERCH

When ice fishing for yellow perch, add a couple of dropper lines (where legal) to your main line. They will definitely increase your catch.

If you are in a boat fishing for early-season yellow perch, the most active fish are often right beside the pack ice that is starting to break up.

Tipping a small jig or spinner with a worm can increase your chances of catching light-biting perch on those "off" days when the fishing is slow.

Early-spring hot spots for yellow perch are shoals and rocky points, particularly when the sun is shining and warming these areas.

If you are planning to use live minnows as bait for perch, make sure they are tiny — no more than 2 inches (5 cm) long. Many anglers use larger minnows and never have more than a few hits in a day.

WHITE BASS

White bass usually swim around in tight schools of several fish of the same size. If the fish you're catching are all small, move to another location and try to find a school that has bigger fish.

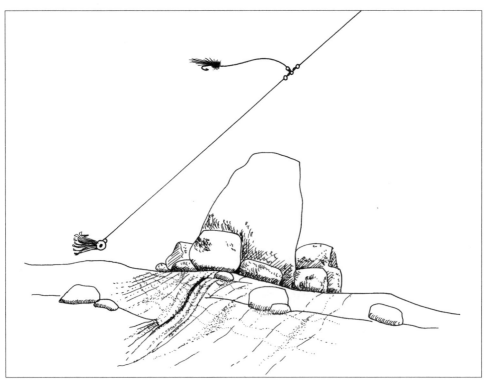

 You can double your pleasure and your results when fishing for white bass if you tie a dropper onto your line and attach a different type of fly or jig than the one already on the line.

 Because light line and small lures are used to catch white bass, it's doubly important to sharpen your hooks. A sharp hook requires less pressure to properly penetrate on the hook set and doesn't put strain on the line.

 Use tiny crankbaits to locate white bass. Once you've locat-ed them, use spoons, spinners, and jigs to catch one fish after the other.

ROCK BASS

 Rock bass are quite tasty and provide a nice meal if you decide to keep a few for the frying pan. They have very few bones to worry about and can be gutted and cooked whole.

 By far the best type of lure for rock bass is a crayfish-imitating jig or crankbait.

- Rock bass are often found with other panfish that will take your lure more quickly. To catch the "rockies," it's sometimes necessary to use a larger lure. If you are using live bait, weight it so that it drops quickly to the bottom, putting it closer to the rock bass.

- Prime lakes for large rock bass populations are those that have an abundance of large gamefish but no smaller ones. In this situation, the rock bass tend to take over as the top predators in shallow water.

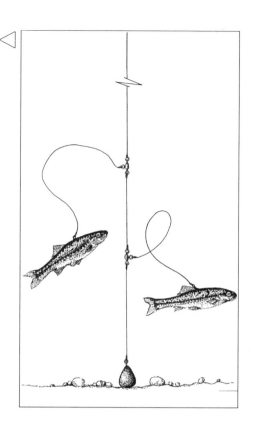

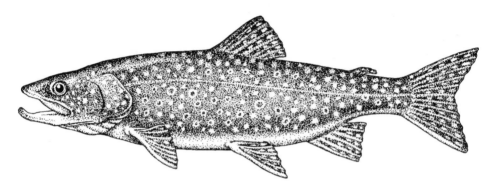

Arctic Char

P O P U L A R   S P E C I E S

··

ARCTIC CHAR, ARCTIC GRAYLING, CHANNEL CATFISH, CUTTHROAT TROUT,
DOLLY VARDEN, INCONNU, PICKEREL, STRIPED BASS, STURGEON

Alternative and Exotic Species

Although bass, walleye, salmon, and trout are the most popular targets for anglers, there are many other species that are slowly entering the limelight for the challenging sport that they provide.

For example, the thundering fight of a channel cat is unparalleled among freshwater species. Exotic fish, such as Arctic grayling, also provide a challenging alternative. The beautiful grayling with its spectacular sail-like dorsal fin is highly prized among anglers who have the opportunity to fish Canada's far north.

The following tips cover a variety of alternative and exotic species for those anglers seeking new challenges.

ARCTIC CHAR

● Always check for char in riffles near the mouths of tributary streams where they like to gather, picking off food as it drifts past. Char often follow a lure for up to 30 feet (9 m) or more before hitting, so leave your bait in the water as long as possible.

● "Spin" fishermen have long been aware of the char's love for brightly flashing spinners and spoons. You can make your own combinations by carrying some self-adhesive prism tape, which is available in a variety of fish-attracting colors. Experiment with different colors until you hit pay dirt.

● Here's a quick tip for the fly angler. If the char are in deep water, you can increase the sinking rate of your fly line by twisting a length of lead core sinking line around the end of the line.

● Fly anglers often use imitation single eggs as attractors on an 18-inch (45-cm) tippet running from the main line. Chartreuse and yellow are the best colors to use. The actual fly is usually a Wooly Bugger or an Egg Sucking Leech. As this rig swings in the current, the char quickly spot the egg. As they close in, they see the larger fly and snap it up.

● One of the most effective egg imitations for char is a simple piece of sponge placed over a bare hook. The sponge can be dyed to almost any color and cut down to any size. It has the added advantage of swirling enticingly in even the slightest eddy or current.

ARCTIC GRAYLING

● One misconception about grayling is that they have soft-tissued mouths. This leads some anglers to set the hook half-heartedly to avoid losing the fish. Unfortunately, it ends up being lightly hooked and lost anyway. To set the record straight, grayling have small but leathery mouths. The hook should be set with a short but firm jerk of the wrist. While playing the fish, maintain steady pressure, keeping the line tight.

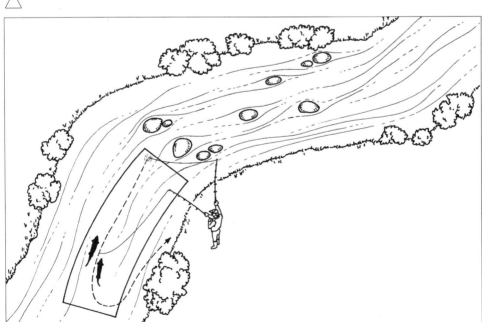

➤ Small spoons are very effective lures when the grayling are resting behind rocks or other current breaks. Stand above the rock or obstruction and cast just upstream from it. Allow the spoon to hang in the current for a moment and then let it flutter down past the hiding fish before tightening the line again. The lure will hover near the fish, drawing strikes where other lures have failed.

- Since grayling love dry flies, make sure your offerings are as good as they can be. Fly anglers often discard dry flies that have become scrawny-looking after a lot of use. This is unnecessary. All you have to do to make them appealing again to grayling is to steam them over a pot of boiling water.

- If the grayling are hitting near the surface on wet flies, here's a tip to make your fly stay near the surface better. Tie a second knot, such as the Portland Creek Half Hitch, directly in front of the fly. This will ensure that it rides on the surface in a manner irresistible to grayling.

- When grayling are less than eager to hit your spinner, try slowing down your presentation. Cast across the stream at right angles to the current. Retrieve slowly enough to allow the current to carry your lure in a slow, tantalizing arc across the tail of the pool.

CHANNEL CATFISH

- Channel catfish take baits very firmly, so there's not much point in letting them run with the bait. Your rod should point at 10 o'clock until a catfish hits the bait. When one does, lower the tip to the water to let the fish take some line and then set the hook hard.

- In the spring, don't overlook dams and other structures for spawning channel cats. It's common to catch ten or fifteen fish a day when they're running heavily. During the day, they hold at the base of dams. As evening approaches, look for them in fast-flowing shallow water.

- In winding rivers, always look for big channel cats in the deepest pools. These are usually found in the bends of the river and often have the added attraction of an undercut bank.

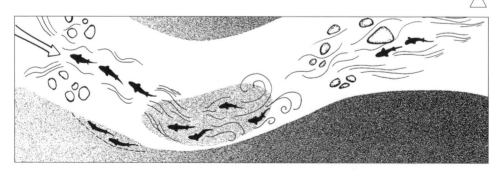

- When the cats aren't biting, try making your presentation more natural by drifting your bait past them. Attach a slip float to your line. As the float drifts downriver, free spool line as necessary to keep the bait just off the bottom, touching the odd rock or boulder. When a fish hits, close the bail and set the hook.

- For a very effective stinkbait, lay some chicken livers out in the sun for a few days. You won't like the aroma, but the channel cats will love it!

CUTTHROAT TROUT

- Because cutthroat trout are so elusive, it is doubly important to fish every structural element or current break as thoroughly as possible.

- When using bait for cutthroat trout, cut your line and leave the hook in a deeply hooked fish that you intend to release. The fish's stomach acids will dissolve the hook. This is much safer than trying to remove a deeply imbedded hook and damaging the fish.

- Giving cutthroat trout a choice of two lures can often bring results. Try tying a 12-inch (30-cm) piece of monofilament to your spoon or spinner and attaching a fly to it. Sometimes only a trailing fly will entice these fish to hit.

- The tiny crankbaits that are so effective for catching cutthroat often need to be weighted with a couple of small split shot to make them dive down closer to feeding fish.

DOLLY VARDEN

- Anglers who fish for Dolly Varden in the fall use salmon roe as bait and a float to register light takers.

- When Dolly Varden are feeding heavily on nymphs, the "spinning" angler can take a tip from the fly fisher and use flies that match the look of nymphs. Although flies are usually too light to use with spinning tackle, the addition of split shot to the line allows you to use them. Simply tie on the proper fly and clamp on some split shot part way up the line.

- Always approach a potential holding spot on a river from downstream. This will ensure that you don't spook the biggest and often the wariest fish.

- When the fishing is slow, tie a bright piece of yarn above your lure to function as an attractor.

- Use flashy flies and lures with erratic actions to catch Dolly Varden consistently.

INCONNU

- Inconnu are much more active on overcast days.

- Hot spots for inconnu are locations where two streams or rivers join together. A normal river flowing into a glacial river is a prime location.

- One of the best ways to locate active inconnu is to look for rolling fish on the surface.

- Because inconnu are known to jump several times during a fight, make sure your hooks are razor-sharp and set the hook several times to ensure adequate hook penetration.

- Inconnu often feed on migrating salmon fingerlings. At this time, fly anglers should "match the hatch" and use flies that match the size and look of the fingerlings. Surprisingly, tarpon flies work well in this situation.

PICKEREL

- Although members of the true pickerel family (as opposed to walleyes, which are often called pickerel) may be small, you still have to handle them with care. After removing the hooks, even small fish should be gently cradled in the water until they have recovered enough to swim away on their own.

- When you are fishing for pickerel in matted weeds, try a frog-imitating surface lure, especially on calm days. You can fish it right over the tops of the weeds to catch some of the big fish that are resting below.

- Because pickerel are voracious feeders, retrieve your spoons or spinners quickly to stimulate aggressive strikes.

- On days when the pickerel are inactive, try enticing them to strike by suspending a 3- to 4-inch (7- to 10-cm) minnow, hooked through the back, below a bobber. Fish it along the edges of heavy weed growth.

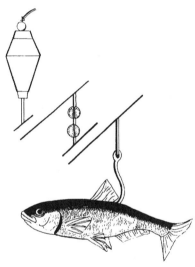

- A good set of needle-nose pliers is a must, even for small pickerel. These aggressive fish can swallow a lure deep inside their tooth-filled mouth.

STRIPED BASS

- To catch particularly large striped bass, use big bait. Eels in the 12- to 18-inch (30- to 45-cm) range will catch some phenomenal fish.

- If you are releasing big striped bass, remove the hooks while the fish is still in the water. Much less stress is put on large fish if they aren't hauled out of the water into the boat.

- As striped bass stop feeding on the surface, be ready to toss a weighted shad-imitating jig into the school. As the lure spirals down, it often moves right through the school and is picked up quickly by one of the bass.

- An erratically retrieved topwater lure will often be savagely attacked when stripers are feeding on the surface.

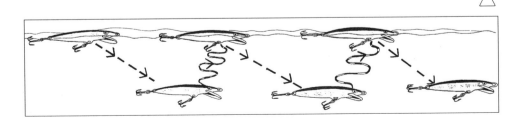

STURGEON

There are a number of different bait rigs for sturgeon fishing, including worms, minnows, and even lamprey eels. Try them all until you find the best rig for the area you are fishing.

Here's a tip for catching very large lake sturgeon. These fish can be found using a sonar unit around river mouths and lake shoals. Once located, a proven walleye technique can be used to catch them. The bait is weighted with an egg sinker and dropped to the bottom. The angler then slowly back trolls, gradually moving the bait around in the sturgeon's feeding grounds until the fish's keen senses locate it.

Lake sturgeons can often be seen rolling in quiet bays of their native lakes. They are also found near the channels and narrows where they feed.

The easiest way to locate white sturgeons is to probe the fast waters below dams and rapids, especially during the spawning season.

Neither lake sturgeons nor white sturgeons hang suspended between the bottom and the top of the water. All your efforts should be concentrated on bait fishing on the bottom.

When using pieces of fish as bait, try shaping them in a way that will make them move enticingly in the current. Sturgeons use their ability to discern small vibrations in the water to find food.

◀ Anglers often use a limp Dacron leader when baitfishing for sturgeons. With this type of leader, the sturgeon's sensitive mouth is less likely to detect that something is wrong and drop the bait.

◀ Experienced sturgeon anglers often use a combination of cut baitfish and two or three worms on their hooks. They then spray WD-40 on the bait. This formula masks human odor and, for some reason, seems to attract these fish.

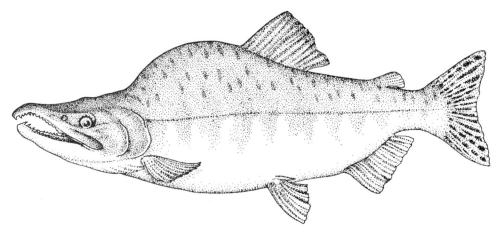

Pink Salmon

COMMON SPECIES
· ·

ATLANTIC SALMON, CHUM SALMON, KOKANEE, PINK SALMON, SOCKEYE SALMON

Alternative Salmon

Much has been written about the popular chinook and coho salmon fishing both in the Great Lakes and on the Pacific coast. There are several other salmon species, however, that provide fantastic sportfishing for anglers from coast to coast.

Atlantic salmon were perhaps the first salmon ever sought by North American anglers. The European discoverers of the east coast found the rivers teeming with fish willing to take flies. The east coast salmon fishery has become a well-protected resource that remains strong even today.

North America's west coast is host to many more salmon — chum, sockeye, kokanee, and pink salmon are all actively pursued by anglers. Pink salmon have even made an appearance in Superior, the largest of the Great Lakes.

ATLANTIC SALMON

Atlantic salmon like to take a fly that appears to be suspended over them. When you identify a feeding lie, cast the fly so that it swings across the current and over the suspected fish. Always suspend the fly in the current directly above the fish for a few moments before retrieving it for another cast.

When dry fly fishing for Atlantics, cast your fly in front and to within a foot (30 cm) of a fish and drift the fly only 2 to 4 feet (60 to 120 cm) past it. If the salmon doesn't take the fly immediately, cast again.

Make sure your flies are presented to the salmon in a broad-side manner. Atlantics can be very finicky takers and will usually ignore flies that they cannot see silhouetted clearly.

Nobody knows exactly what prompts an Atlantic salmon to hit flies. They are unpredictable and may strike a fly at any time. For this reason, make sure you cast to this fish in a persistent manner. Casts should be made to a visible fish about 20 or 30 times. If the fish doesn't seem interested, don't give up too quickly!

Atlantic salmon are renowned the world over for their excellent fighting qualities. Fly anglers often use extension butts, which pop into the bottom of their fly rods. These "fighting" butts give the angler much more leverage during a fight and are particularly useful for battling salmon in fast water.

Many fly anglers also troll flies for ouananiche, the landlocked version of the Atlantic salmon. Two basic streamer fly types are tied to a full sinking line. Tandem streamers are made by joining two long shank hooks with a short piece of monofilament line. These tandem designs are easy to tie, track through the water easily, and increase hook-setting ability. Single streamers are much lighter, more natural-looking, and easier to present under certain conditions, but they suffer from a diminished hook-setting ability, especially for timid strikes that often fall short of the hook.

CHUM SALMON

◖ When the chum arrive around river mouths to spawn in late fall, they will take artificial lures, such as wobbling plugs. The secret is to use lures with patterns that contain red or fluorescent orange.

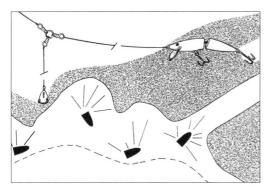

◖ To increase the appeal of your egg baits, add a piece of brightly colored Styrofoam, such as the Li'l Corky, above the hook. These tiny balls, which resemble single eggs, will also increase the buoyancy of your roe bag, keeping it from snagging on the bottom.

◖ Chum salmon are egg eaters and what better bait than natural roe? Even chunks of roe with the skein still attached are a highly effective bait. Anglers

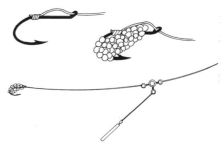

often pass the line through the eye of the hook and snell it on to the hook bend. This creates a kind of loop between the eye and the bend that can be tightened around the hooked roe chunk to keep it from falling off the hook.

◖ Chum are often found in small pockets or runs that cannot be drift fished because of their size and the many nearby rocks. Don't pass up these tiny holding pools. In such close confines, simply step near the pocket, pull out a short length of line, and dunk the bait vertically into the hole.

KOKANEE SALMON

◖ When you are trolling river inlets for kokanee, it sometimes helps to use a planer board to take your lure out and away from the boat. This is particularly useful on bright days in very clear water conditions when the fish are spooky.

- When fishing for kokanee in dirty water, try using a rattling crankbait to help the fish home in on your lure. A vibrating spinner like the Blue Fox Vibrax is also a top choice in dirty water conditions.

- Think small when selecting lures for kokanee. Too many anglers use big artificial lures, which are unappealing to these insect- and plankton-eating fish.

- The best time to find and catch aggressively feeding kokanee salmon is just after ice-out.

- Jigging with a tear-drop jig imitates the movement of the invertebrates that make up the bulk of a kokanee's diet.

PINK SALMON

- When the pinks enter a river to spawn, roe bags are a good bait to use. If the water is dirty from a heavy rain, the salmon will still hit if you make your offering more visible. This can be done by sliding a very bright plastic egg onto the line just above the hook's eye. Add an oversized, bright spawn sac and your "dirty-water special" will be complete.

- If you are using a float with a spawn bag to catch pinks, always use a leader of light line below the float. The light leader is usually tied onto a swivel, which prevents line twist. If your bag snags up, the leader will break first, saving your float.

- When the water is very clear, single salmon eggs on light line are deadly for pinks, especially if there are spawning chinooks or cohos nearby. Because single fresh eggs can break apart on the hook, boil them first until they become firm.

- You can increase your odds of hooking hungry river pinks by throwing a handful of loose eggs into the pool before casting your roe bag or single egg.

- When using a small fly to catch pinks, try suspending it from a tiny float so that the fly just barely clears the bottom. Use a brightly colored fly pattern and keep your eyes glued on the float; it will serve as a strike indicator when a fish hits.

SOCKEYE SALMON

- The most productive time of the year to fish for sockeye salmon is when they are scattered in the rivers just prior to forming schools for spawning.

- Sockeye feed on a variety of small invertebrates. You will have consistent catches if you use small lures, such as spinners, spoons, and crankbaits.

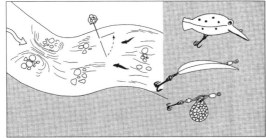

- Because sockeye are soft hitters, you must have very sharp hooks for proper penetration.

- Sockeye don't feed once they have entered rivers to spawn, but anglers can still fool them. Fish imprint on the prey they fed on as fingerlings in the river. A well-presented fly that imitates the forage of their youth can often trigger sockeye into striking.

- Sockeye can be spunky, so you should use a tailing glove, such as Normark's Fillet Glove, to handle the fish more easily.

Fighting and Landing Fish

Many anglers hook trophy fish each year but, for one reason or another, seem to lose them on a regular basis. Hooking a fish is just the beginning. Knowing how to fight and land one properly is equally important.

One of the most important factors in fighting fish is your reel's drag. Some anglers have their drags set improperly or don't use them at all. Others get so excited when they hook a fish that they try to land it as quickly as possible and end up losing it.

The final act of landing fish should also be mastered. Many fish are fought and then lost at the last minute near the shore or boat. Everyone who's spent any time fishing from a boat has probably had the disappointing experience of losing a big fish. The following tips will help you successfully land trophy fish and keep your losses to a minimum.

Never fight a trophy fish from a boat without first lifting fish stringers and anchors into the boat. Fish will often try to wrap the line around various objects and even around the lower unit of the outboard motor.

Most people don't realize how important it is to achieve a good hook set. It's not enough just to snap the rod back to set the hook. It's just as important to keep a lot of tension on the line and to crank the reel several times so that the hook point will penetrate beyond the barb.

As soon as a large fish is hooked in open water, it's a good idea to loosen the drag slightly. As the fish begins to tire, tighten the drag to begin forcing it toward the boat.

After you have hooked a fish in fast water, lessen the rod pressure allowing the fish to move downstream into your open net. Submerge two-thirds of the net so that the current opens the net mesh wide. Make sure the fish enters head-first.

In a current, always try to move downstream from a fighting fish. This will give you more control over the fish and, because it will fight its way upstream, the odds of the hook being pulled out of its mouth are decreased.

The smoothest drag for fighting a fish is a manual one. By controlling the line's drag with your fingers, you can let the fish take as much or as little line as you want.

If you are fighting fish that tend to jump out of the water, such as bass, musky, or trout, place the rod tip below the water's surface when you see the fish heading quickly toward the surface and you anticipate a jump. This will discourage the fish from making several jumps.

If a hooked fish wants to run, don't force it to stop. Very often taking some of the pressure off the fish will make it slow down and stop taking out line.

When you're confronted with a jumping fish, lower the rod toward the fish, creating controlled slack in the line. As the fish falls back into the water, you can gain control once again by raising the rod. This technique is called "bowing a fish."

When fighting bass and other gamefish in heavy cover, try to keep the fish's head close to the surface so it can't dive into the cover and become entangled.

- When fighting a fish, it's important to hold the rod high in the air. This maximizes the pressure put on the fish.

- Remember, never crank your reel when a fish is running off drag; your line can get twisted.

- There are a few key instructions to remember when landing a fish after it has tripped the downrigger release. Set the hook and keep your rod tip up high. Don't crank the reel when the fish runs line out; instead, slowly "pump" your fish with the use of the rod. And, finally, don't bring your fish by the net when it's still "green," or lively.

- Always net a fish that has been lightly hooked on an artificial lure tail-first. This will decrease the chances of getting the

hooks caught in the net. If the fish is hooked deeply, however, a head-first scoop with the net is fine.

- Landing nets often undergo a beating during a fishing trip and need repair. Use an ordinary garbage bag tie to mend the hole until you can repair it properly.

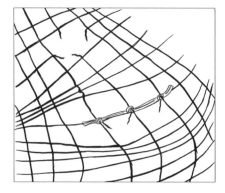

▽

 Nets with large rubber strands are better than those made of twine or cotton. It is easier to remove hooks from this type of net, and it will last longer, too.

 Dip the net completely underwater prior to netting your trophy. Lead the fish into the net instead of stabbing at it with the net.

 Place Styrofoam chips in your net handles. If the net flips overboard, it will float and you can go back and pick it up.

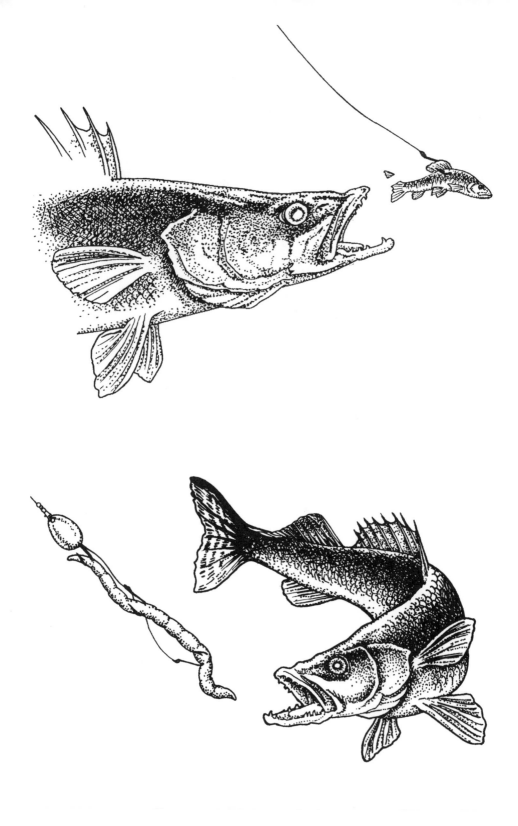

Fishing with Live Bait

There is a significant difference between fishing natural bait effectively and just "soaking" it. One key word that comes to mind is "presentation." The bait must be hooked properly and put in front of the fish in a realistic manner.

Many anglers like to use a lighter weight line to make the bait appear more natural in the water. The same holds true for terminal tackle, such as hooks and weights. Nine times out of ten, the angler should use the smallest hook possible.

The following guidelines will help you catch, preserve, and use live bait, no matter what species of fish you're planning to catch.

➤ Getting snagged over rocks occurs quite frequently when bait fishing. Adding a slip bobber to your line and adjusting the depth so that your bait hangs just above the rocks will eliminate this problem.

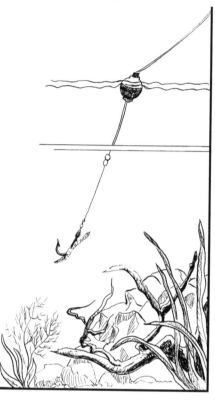

➤ When using live bait, keep your bait as fresh and active as possible; use the lightest line possible; present the bait in a natural manner; and stay alert and be ready to set the hook.

➤ You can easily catch bait for walleyes and smallmouths by sinking empty beer or pop cans strung together on a line in a weedy river or shallow lake overnight. Minnows, crayfish, and even small catfish will hide in the cans. Simply retrieve the cans the next morning for a day's supply of bait.

➤ Stinger hooks work well with live bait when fish are hitting lightly. Insert one hook into the head of the bait and the other into the tail. Many fishermen have used this technique with worms for years, but try stinger hooks on your minnows, salamanders, even frogs when the fish are biting short.

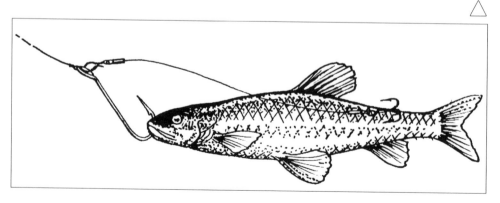

Use three-way swivels to effectively present your live bait when using more than one hook. This will keep the extra baited hooks from tangling with the main line.

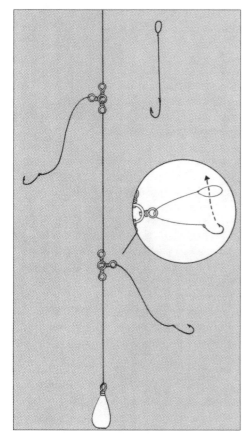

One of the best live-bait rigs is called the "double bobbin' rig." It involves rigging two different live baits on the same line under a float or bobber. This allows two different presentations on a single line and may double your catch in a hurry.

Terminal tackle for bait fishing is very important; however, remember not to use too much. You should be able to feel every nibble. Also, allow at least 18 inches (45 cm) of line between the bait and the sinkers so that the bait drifts in the current in a natural way.

If a dew worm refuses to be pulled out of the ground, don't yank it. Instead, apply steady pressure; the worm will eventually tire and slide out of its hole.

In wooded areas, look for worms under logs and rocks, especially after rain. Don't be surprised if you find some salamanders, too.

Use a barrel sinker and floating jig head to suspend live bait off the bottom where it is more visible to feeding fish.

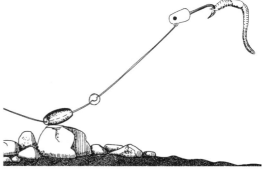

If you put red brick dust in your worm box bedding, the worms will be richer in color within a few days, making them more attractive to the fish.

Use a flashlight with red cellophane over the lens when gathering dew worms. White light makes them go back into their holes.

Driving over rough roads can affect live bait, especially worms. Continuous vibrations can damage or even kill them before you arrive at your fishing spot. Put your bait boxes either on your car seat or boat cushion. Minnows react in the same way. Make sure you have plenty of water in their bucket so that they don't bounce against the sides too much.

Keeping dew worms fresh and wriggly is sometimes a problem. Placing a few ice cubes into their bedding during hot weather will help, and if you can persuade the family to let you use the refrigerator between fishing trips, your worms will stay healthy in their container until needed.

Worms are more attractive to fish if they are clean. Place them in some damp moss a few days prior to a fishing trip and they'll get rid of the dirt in their bodies.

A good time to get your supply of dew worms is after a heavy rain. The worms cover sidewalks and roads by the hundreds. A spatula is a good

pickup tool. When you have enough, store them in your worm box.

An excellent bait for trout is water worms (crane fly larvae). If you hook them lightly, they'll flip back and forth as you drift fish, enticing the most stubborn trout to bite. Try locating these worms in the mud and sticks of beaver dams.

To keep grasshoppers and other insects alive on your hook

longer, don't pierce their body with the hook. Instead, attach them to the hook with a small elastic.

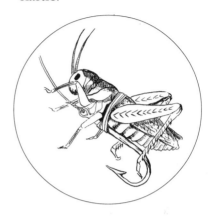

If you have access to a woodpile, you may have a decent supply of ice-fishing bait. Look for some pieces of punky wood and split them. Holes in rotten wood often contain golden grubs, sometimes as long as a ½-inch (1.2 cm). Several dozen grubs can be located in a short period of time.

Leeches can be easily caught. Place some rocks inside a large coffee can to hold it down underwater, add some fresh fish heads, and put the top on. Make some small slits on each end of the can for the leeches to enter. Sink the can in a pond, marsh, or bog. The best time to remove the leeches from the can is before the sun comes up.

- Two or three aspirins in your minnow bucket may keep your minnows alive until you can change their water.

- To keep minnows alive during hot weather, punch several holes in a plastic bag, fill it with ice, and tie the top closed. Hang the bag over your minnow bucket. As the ice melts, cool water will drip into the bucket and keep the water from over-heating.

- Frogs can be easily caught. Shine a flashlight directly on them in late evening. This temporarily mesmerizes them. Slowly move in and grab them or, better yet, net them. If your reflexes are too slow, use a fly swatter. A light tap will enable you to put them in your bucket, where they'll come to shortly afterward.

- Old pairs of pantyhose are great for gathering grasshoppers in open fields. Simply drag them behind you while walking at a moderate speed and you will eventually have a whole mess of grasshoppers tangled in the nylon. All you have to do is pick them off and place them in your bait bucket.

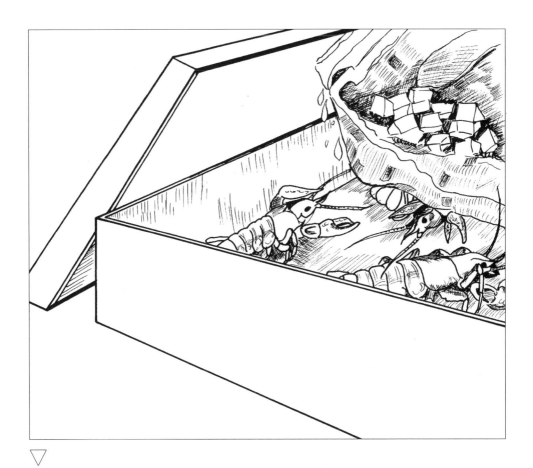

$\triangledown$

- Although crayfish live in water, it's not necessary to keep them in water while on a fishing trip. They will stay alive and fresh for quite some time in a bait box lined with moss or even damp newspaper. Ice cubes will help keep them active in hot weather.

- An effective way to catch frogs is to "fish" for them. Tie an artificial fly to your fishing line, dangle it in front of a frog, and hold on!

- Many anglers use crayfish for bass fishing, yet small crayfish up to an inch (about 2 cm) long can make excellent bait for trout. These small crayfish are sometimes hard to locate, so try using the tails of the larger ones. Float them along the bottom in deep pools and runs.

Catch and Release Fishing

ne of the most talked-about philosophies in the art of fishing is the concept of live release. Releasing most or all of the fish you catch is becoming much more popular. That is not to say that catch and release fishing wasn't practiced in the 1600s when Izaak Walton was delicately presenting caddis fly imitations to rising trout. Indeed, fly anglers have long been consummate live-release anglers.

Live-release fishing, however, has taken on much greater importance with the decline of fish stocks. In fact, catch and release laws have now been passed in many jurisdictions. Maximum keep limits, slot limits (which allow anglers to keep only smaller-sized fish and perhaps one trophy), and barbless hook regulations are all being used to help ensure healthy fish populations.

The following tips will show you how to handle the fish that you catch safely and carefully so you too can help to protect our precious gamefish for generations to come.

One of the best catch and release tools is a camera. Everyone likes to brag about the "big one" that was released. Rather than killing the fish as proof, a photograph can provide the evidence.

Killing fish just to mount them on the wall is slowly becoming a thing of the past. Now you can take a picture and the measurements of your trophy and get a replica mount made. Replicas are highly detailed right down to the scale markings.

If you intend to release fish you catch, don't use the lightest line available. This prolongs the fight and increases the chances of the fish dying.

Panfish enthusiasts often keep only the largest of the fish they catch for the table. However, in threatened fisheries, live-release advocates are now stressing the need to release the largest fish. These genetically superior fish should be protected so that they can continue to spawn.

If you intend to release a trophy fish, especially a big lake trout, pike, or musky, never lift it vertically out of the water. This causes damage to the internal organs.

If you have to pick up a large fish that you intend to release, make sure that you support it in the mid-section to prevent internal damage.

One of the safest tools to use for landing big fish is the catch and release cradle. It consists of a piece of soft cotton mesh stretched between two long slender pieces of wood to form something resembling a stretcher. A large fish can safely be led into the cradle beside the boat, and the fish's weight can then be supported when it and the cradle are lifted aboard.

Needle-nose pliers are one of the best tools for the catch and release angler. If you fish from a boat, you need never actually lift the fish into the boat. Simply bring it alongside and remove the hooks with the pliers as the fish rests in the water.

Nets can do a lot of damage to fish and are becoming unpopular among catch and release anglers. If you have to use a net to land a fish you intend to release, a rubber-coated mesh one is better than one made of multistrand nylon. The flexible rubber mesh landing nets made by Lucky Strike are the best.

Digital scales are handy to have with you on fishing trips to measure the fish that you intend to release. You can take a picture of your fish hanging on the scale to prove to everyone back home how big it really was. If you use a cradle, simply subtract the cradle's weight from the total weight of the cradle and the fish.

$\triangledown$

The safest way to handle trout and salmon when you are stream fishing is to tail the fish and leave it in the water while the hook is removed. Tailing is accomplished by firmly grasping the fish by the narrow section of the body just ahead of the tail, which is called the caudal peduncle.

Never hold a fish under the gills. This will almost certainly damage the fish and lead to its eventual death.

Many anglers simply toss bass and other fish back into the water. This can cause irreparable damage, especially to their sensitive gills. Take a moment to reach down and gently slide the fish back into the water.

If you are going to release your fish, don't fight it for a long time. Try to bring it to the boat as quickly as you can and then go through the proper release methods.

The safest way to retrieve a fish that you intend to release is to cradle it in the water and gently move it forward, *not backward*, in the water. A fish's gills can be damaged when it is moved backward.

- Anglers who have live wells to keep stressed-out fish in good condition until they are ready to go home should use live well chemicals such as Catch & Release. This chemical is designed to protect fish against viral infection and to relieve stress.

- Making your own portable live well is easy. All you need is a camping cooler of suitable size, a bilge pump, a 3-foot (90-cm) length of car heater hose, and suction cups. Screw the suction cups to the bottom of the pump so that it can be mounted on the inside of the cooler. To fill your live well, attach the heater hose to the bilge pump and put the pump over the side of the boat. Then pump fresh water into the cooler. When it is filled, take the hose off and mount the pump just under the water surface in the cooler so that the water is circulated continuously. To empty the cooler, again attach the hose to the pump and use the bilge pump to return the water to the lake.

- On very hot days, adding a chunk or block of ice to your live well will help decrease the oxygen demands of your fish and keep them in better condition.

Fly Fishing

The special group of anglers who enjoy fishing with an artificial fly or insect spend many hours perfecting their sense of rhythm, timing, and presentation. Unfortunately, for this reason, fly fishing has had the reputation of being too difficult to master, but with a little practice any angler can become successful at this sport. Like any other type of fishing, choosing the proper tackle is of great importance.

Serious fly anglers study insects and when they hatch in the water to determine which flies to use. This usually also influences casting techniques, which are designed to convince even the most stubborn fish to hit.

Fly fishing can be fun for catching a number of species, but browns, rainbows, brook trout, and salmon top the list.

Felt or indoor/outdoor carpeting cemented to the soles of waders helps you wade quietly as well as safely. It allows you to approach a fish holding spot without disturbing a potential catch.

When fly fishing for a particular species, the selection of tackle should reflect the size of the fly, the type and size of the water to be fished, and the average size of the fish in that water.

Nylon lines can be left on reel spools from season to season without harm. If any tight coils develop over the winter, they can be removed by stretching the line.

Mangled dry flies can be made to look as good as new by holding them with pliers over a steaming kettle.

When dry flies don't work during a hatch, a small streamer fly sometimes does. Fish try to drive away competitors, and streamers look just like minnows or other intruders.

A shock tippet of 40-pound test monofilament will help you land more pike using flies. Tie a 1-foot (30-cm) section between the leader and the fly.

If some of your dry flies become so chewed that they no longer float well, just trim them into the shape of a nymph and fish them that way.

Fly anglers who walk through the bush to their favorite fishing spots will find shoe/stocking foot waders particularly useful. The waders fold into a small package and can be put on when you reach the water.

Use a 12-pound test leader tip when you are fishing for bass in heavy weed cover. You'll need it to pull the bigmouths out to open water.

- Always match the fly reel with the line weight of the rod. For example, for a 2 to 4 weight rod, use a small reel; for a 4 to 7 weight rod, a medium reel; and for a 7 to 12 weight rod, a large reel.

- On sunny days, fish the shady side of the river, right up against the bank. That's usually where the trout will hold.

- A clean floating line will cast 10 to 20 yards (9 to 18 m) further than a dirty line.

- Experienced salmon fly anglers use simple hair-wing or tube-fly patterned flies in a very limited range of colors. In fact, a black fly with a small colored butt is all that is usually needed to entice the spawning fish to hit.

- Many fly anglers use plastic compartmentalized boxes to house their dry flies. If you fasten small strips of magnetic tape to the bottom, your hooks will stay in place until you're ready to use them.

- Polaroid sunglasses will help you spot fish and the best underwater areas to cast to.

- When tying nymphs, weight some with enough lead to send them to the bottom and leave others to float near the surface.

- Don't assume that the largest insect is the one the trout are taking during a hatch. Often the smaller insects that are present in greater numbers are the better choice.

- A stiff monofilament weed guard on a bass bug will let you fish heavily weeded waters. Remember to point the rod at the fly during the slow retrieve.

- A strong but light leader for sharp-toothed fish can be made from thin piano wire, which is available at your local music store.

- Fly "mud" can be used to sink your line deeper. Apply it to sections of your line that should sink quickly.

If you're planning to use wet or dry flies on a favorite stream or river, hang a piece or strip of flypaper on a tree near the stream for a few hours. When you return, the kinds of flies trapped on the flypaper will give you a good idea of what kind of artificial flies you should use.

Sharpen your hooks religiously. After several takes without the fish being hooked, it's time to check the hook's sharpness.

Always check your rod guides for chips and rough edges. These will destroy expensive fly lines. Replace the damaged guides when necessary.

For heavy-action fly fishing for Atlantic salmon, Pacific salmon, and other large fish, the fly reel should have a rim spool. This type of spool allows anglers to "palm" the reel when they are fighting a large fish. Your palm, held against the spool's rim, acts as a drag.

- Many fly anglers have experienced tremendous fall smallmouth bass action by casting to shoreline structures in shallow water on warm sunny days and by casting to submerged points in deeper water on colder days.

- Carry your camera in a large self-sealing plastic bag or waterproof container. If you happen to fall into the water, the camera will stay dry and you will still be able to take a few pictures of your trophy trout before going home.

- When you are fishing deeper holes and runs with medium-sinking fly lines, try adding a length of lead core line to the end of your fly line. It will sink your line automatically.

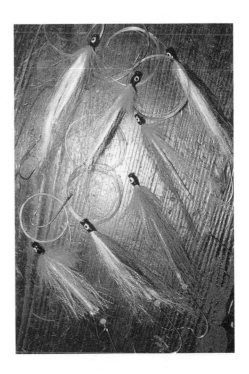

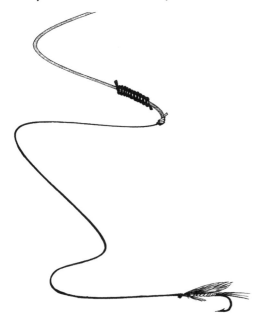

- Fly anglers are well equipped to catch spring steelhead. Once steelhead finish spawning, they revert back to their bright silver colors and start feeding voraciously. It's at this time that streamers, wet flies, and nymphs work well.

- Many anglers tie their flies along a stream as soon as they learn which live insects the trout are feeding on.

- Use a short 6-foot (1.8-m) leader when you are fishing with big flies in murky water. The fish won't see the leader and the fly will stay close to the strike zone near the bottom.

If you want to make your weight-forward sinking fly line sink even faster, cut the first few feet (less than a meter) off the lead and tie your leader to the heaviest part of the taper.

The key to reading water for all fish is to locate areas in rivers, lakes, and streams where food is concentrated. In rivers, fish the heads of pools and deep runs; in lakes, fish the points, shoals, and drop-offs.

Fly-line "dressing" will help make your fly line and leader float much better, especially through fast, rolling water areas.

Most fly-line backing should be changed every few months if used continuously.

Use Armor All to re-condition old fly lines. Just pour some on a cloth and pass your chafed line through it.

A fly reel should never be over-filled with backing and line. As a rule of thumb, allow a quarter inch (50 mm) of empty space on your spool.

To straighten your leader, use a piece of chamois rather than a rubber inner tube. The chamois creates less heat and does not damage the monofilament.

Use Dacron rather than nylon backing on a fly reel. It doesn't stretch under the pressure of fighting a large fish. When wound onto the reel, stretched nylon can break the reel.

A stream diary is very important when you are fly fishing. In it are kept notes on daily fishing excursions, the flies used, fish taken, and any other facts that can provide help on a return fishing trip. Most of all, it will remind you which flies need to be tied before the next trip.

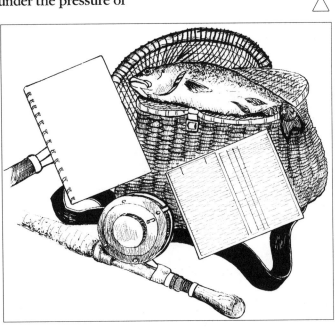

Ice Fishing

Ice fishing is an enjoyable way to pass the winter months and has grown in popularity, particularly in the last decade. Ice hut operators provide the average angler with shelter and advice on thousands of lakes throughout North America.

There are only two requirements for winter fishing. You need a lake with fish in it and sufficient ice to be able to travel safely on the lake. To increase your enjoyment, learn about the ice conditions in your area, ice-fishing tackle and equipment, how to locate fish through the ice, and fishing techniques. You'll find that ice fishing is probably the easiest and most sociable type of fishing there is. It is also one of the cheapest — and your catch won't spoil!

When you have drilled a number of holes for a weekend of ice fishing, remember to place a branch across each unused hole. The branches will prevent other fishermen from stepping into the holes and will help you find the holes the next day.

Extra holes usually pay off. Move your tip-ups from hole to hole until you find a productive area, then cluster the tip-ups around that one area.

Drilling holes through the ice to check depths is tedious. An electronic depth-sounder and a transducer can save a lot of work. Just put your transducer in a plastic bag filled with antifreeze and place it on top of the ice. Your depth reading should be quite accurate.

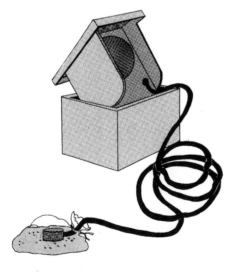

When looking for productive pike locations, check your hydrographic map to find an underwater point, then drill several holes from shallow to deeper water. This method allows you to fish different depths systematically until you locate the fish.

When you are ice fishing on an unfamiliar lake, start with a triangle formation of holes about 50 feet (15 m) apart. It will give you a good idea of the water depth and vegetation. Repeat this pattern until you find fish.

Because many winter fish travel in schools, it's often wise to have several ice holes ready at the same time. As the school moves by each one, your tip-ups will fly up and down during the feeding frenzy.

If you're able to clear the snow around the hole, do so. The added light will attract fish.

Few people think of taking a flasher unit on the ice; however, there are several portable models available for the dedicated ice fisherman. With one of these units, you can determine water depth, the amount of vegetation on the bottom, and any fish that may be present, all

without cutting a single hole. Simply clear the snow or slush off the surface of the ice and make sure the transducer is in solid contact with the ice surface. The unit will work "through" the ice.

➤ If you are unaware of shoreline structure, a hydrographic map will help.

➤ To keep your ice hole open in cold weather, drill a second hole several inches (several centimeters) deep next to your fishing hole. Place a large can of lit charcoal briquettes in the shallow hole. It will warm the water in the fishing hole and keep it from freezing over.

➤ If you are fishing on ice that is covered with snow patches, make your holes in these snowy areas. Fish in shallow water will sometimes use snow patches as cover. The snow will also provide better traction for running from hole to hole.

➤ Make sure that your fishing hole is smooth around the edges. If the edges are too irregular, your fishing line may fray and break during a fight with a good-sized fish.

➤ On extremely cold winter days when the snow is constantly being blown into your hole, don't clean it away immediately. It will help keep the hole open.

water 6 inches to 1 foot (15 to 30 cm) high on the windward side of the hole. This will make the snow drift around the hole.

- If you locate a drop-off around a point of land, place your holes along its curve with the odd one located in deeper water. You then have the choice of fishing shallow or deep as the fish move around the point.

- If you've never used an ice auger, you don't know what you're missing. Not only can you cut the hole more quickly with an auger, but you can also make a smoother opening. If you want to cut six or more holes during the day, an auger will give you more time to enjoy fishing.

- When you are fishing two holes within a certain area on the lake, be sure to check local regulations on the maximum distance you are allowed to be from your fishing line.

- Before using an ice spud or ax to make your ice-fishing hole, attach a thin rope to the handle and tie it around your wrist. This safety strap will prevent your tool from going to the bottom of the lake when you cut through the last layer of ice.

- On very windy days, keep snow from filling in your hole by building a wall of snow and

- Be careful never to drop your auger on the ice or road. The blades can become damaged very quickly and are expensive to replace. Always use a cover over the blades. To make one, take some rubber hose and slit it up the middle. Place the hose over the blades and use elastics to keep it there. The cover will protect your vehicle and your hands as well as the auger.

- The larger the auger diameter, the greater the chance that the blades will slip when you are trying to cut a hole. Most ice fishermen will agree that 6- to 8-foot (1.8- to 2.4-m) diameter holes are large enough for most types of gamefish.

- If your auger starts slipping, the blades may be iced up. Make sure you take a rag with you on the ice so that you can wipe the blades carefully whenever you finish digging a hole.

- Dull auger blades can be honed on the ice with a pocketknife or a portable steel. Run the metal on both sides of the blades to bring the edge back.

- The most productive fishing areas are located near weed beds, underwater springs, and where wind has blown away the snow.

- The most productive time to ice fish is when a lake first freezes over in the winter.

- A particular area on a lake may be productive for a number of weeks during the winter. Be sure to mark your hot spot with a branch so that you can find the spot easily on your return.

- Increase your fishing success by chumming a hole. You can make chum from a mixture of items, including ground-up pieces of worm, fish, and meat. Add some crushed eggshells and dry oatmeal or cooked barley and get set for some hot fishing action.

- You can over-chum an area. Make sure you don't saturate your fishing hole with food for the fish that you want to entice.

- Chumming a hole attracts minnows and other baitfish. This in turn attracts larger gamefish.

A chum pot can be made quite easily from an empty bleach jug. Just drill ¼-inch (50-mm) holes into the jug, fill it with chum, and hang it in the hole.

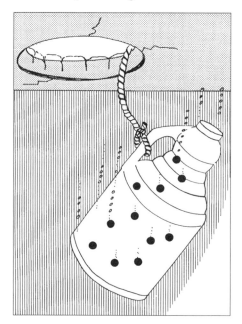

Always tip your spoons with minnows. Hook the minnow between the eyes, making sure the barb is exposed. When using a minnow-tipped spoon, be careful you don't rip the minnow off by jigging too roughly.

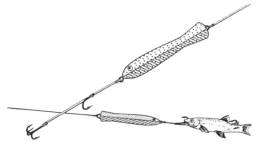

Never let minnows dangle in the cold air for a long period of time. They can freeze very quickly, and to attract gamefish, they should be alive. After you hook a minnow, hold it in your hand until you reach the hole, then slip it gently into the water. The minnow should try to swim away.

Never kill your minnows at the end of a day of ice fishing. In the winter, minnows can be kept alive in a garage, fruit cellar, or basement for weeks if the temperature is cool and the water is changed occasionally.

Don't throw away dead or injured minnows. Freeze them and take them with you on your next trip to tip your spoons and jigs.

If you are planning to go to a small trout lake to fish, first check the local fishing regulations. Fishermen are not allowed to use live minnows as bait on many smaller lakes.

Styrofoam or plastic pails are much better for holding your minnows than metal buckets. The water in metal buckets freezes faster than the water in Styrofoam pails.

- A Styrofoam cooler will also help keep your minnows from freezing.

- One way to hook a minnow is to place the hook just under the skin along one side of the dorsal fin instead of right through the body. The baitfish will remain alive longer as well as be more active.

- Cheap minnow buckets made of foam tend to break at the rope handles. To make them last longer, pull the knots on the handle down 1 inch (2.5 cm) on each side and wrap electrical tape around the bucket above the knots a couple of times. All the weight will then be on the tape.

- To make dead minnows look alive, attach a piece of foil or cardboard to the tip of a twig. As the wind hits the foil, it will move the twig and the minnow from side to side.

- When ice fishing waters with a current, use heavier weights to keep your bait down. The most common rig is a pickerel rig weighted down with a bell sinker.

- Small $\frac{1}{16}$-ounce (1.75-g) jigs are great for perch, but you'll need larger $\frac{1}{4}$-ounce (7-g) jigs for walleyes and lake trout. You can dress your jigs with minnows.

- To catch trophy lake trout in a lake containing whitefish and lake herrings, catch some of these baitfish and use them as bait.

- When you are ice fishing for lake trout, try fishing at various depths, including on the bottom. Dead baits fished on the bottom sometimes produce some of the largest lake trout.

- For shallow water, the best live-bait rig is simply split shot and a hook.

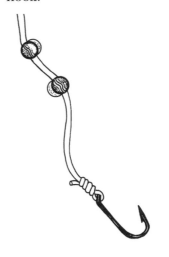

When you are ice fishing with live bait for walleyes, don't set the hook hard when a bite occurs. Instead, start bringing the line in with firm, steady pressure. Walleyes will often close their mouths on a minnow and won't open them until they are flopped onto the ice.

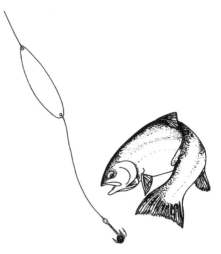

In many jurisdictions, it's legal to use two hooks on one line. When you are ice fishing, use this to your advantage. A fish will often miss the first minnow but will be hooked on the second one. When using two minnows, never pull up your rig immediately after losing a fish. Wait a few minutes to see if the fish takes the second hook.

In colder weather, walleyes sometimes like slow-moving lures (jigs and minnows), jigging Rapalas, and light spoons (Williams Wablers and flutter spoons). In milder weather, they tend to strike fast-dropping spoons, such as the Mr. Champ, Alligator, Little Cleo, and Rapala Pilki spoons. Try sizes from $\frac{1}{4}$ to $\frac{1}{2}$ ounce (7 to 14 g).

One of the best artificial baits for lake herrings is a flashing spoon with a leader 6 to 10 inches (15 to 25 cm) long tied to the bottom split ring in place

of the treble hook. At the end of the leader, attach a small treble with a "pearl" attached to it. The spoon resembles a herring chasing food (the "pearl"). This excites other herrings, making them strike.

Speckles (brook trout) like flashy spoons that are $\frac{1}{8}$ to $\frac{1}{16}$ ounce (3.5 to 1.75 g) in size. Small spinners (sizes 0 to 2) tipped with a piece of worm also work well.

Whitefish take the smallest baits. Swedish Pimples and Mr. Champs in the $\frac{1}{16}$ and $\frac{1}{32}$ ounce (1.75 g to 0.8 g) range are favorites. Russian type tear-drop jigs are also high producers.

Lake trout spoons should be $\frac{1}{4}$ to $1\frac{1}{2}$ ounce (7 to 42 g) in size. Large, flashy spoons with erratic actions work well. Airplane jigs and large homemade plugs jigged vertically catch many trophy lake trout each year.

- Floats work well in ice holes; however, watch your float continuously and be sure to break the ice if it freezes around the float. A float makes it easy to change fishing depths and to detect the slightest hit even under windy conditions.

- Ice fishing for steelhead is becoming popular near river mouths that have open seasons all year long. Anglers jig spoons or roe near the bottom for the best results. Try propping up a tarpaulin over your head to increase the visibility under the ice.

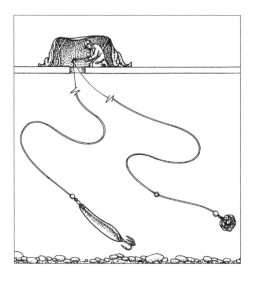

- If you are fishing for perch, walleyes, herrings, speckled trout, and small lake trout, 6- to 10-pound test line is strong enough. If you are fishing for pike or large walleyes and lake trout, use 14- to 25-pound test line.

- Many anglers use heavy monofilament lines for ice fishing because they believe lines get stiffer and weaker in the cold. The line does become stiffer but not weaker. Monofilament line is actually strongest in cold weather.

- Herrings travel in large schools and constantly roam. If you are herring fishing and start catching fish, fish as hard as you can while the fish are present. The fishing is usually fast and sweet but can end at any moment as the school moves away.

- When fishing for whitefish, use an extremely sensitive tip-up and balance it on the stand. Watch for the slightest movement. A bite may pull the line down, but the line may also simply go slack.

- If you lose your ice-fishing ladle, use a kitchen sieve to scoop out slush and pieces of ice from your hole.

Many anglers use Dacron braided line for ice fishing at greater depths for lake trout. They prefer the Dacron line because it has less stretch and will remain straighter under the water, making it easier to determine when the lure or bait is on the bottom.

Most fishermen use a short ice fishing rod for jigging. Normark has several models on the market designed for small fish as well as for trophy lakers and pike.

Even in winter, walleye fishing is best at night. Many ice fishermen leave the lake too early. Some of the best fishing occurs when it's too dark to see your tip-up flags.

To locate herrings, start jigging on the bottom then walk away from the hole while you are jigging. Stop at 10-foot (3-m) intervals, keeping track of the depth in this way. As soon as you start catching fish, work that depth thoroughly.

Don't throw away your broken fishing rod. Save it and cut it down to 2 to 4 feet (60 to 120 cm) in length. Add a new tip and you will have an ideal ice-fishing rod.

When the lake is frozen over, walk along the ice near banks or road bridges that are fished heavily in the summer and look for lures hanging in the trees. You'll find plenty after the leaves have fallen off.

Use the lightest line possible for your target species. For perch, 4-pound test works well, while 8- to 12-pound line is best for walleyes and lake trout.

Many ice fishermen and winter steelhead anglers snip the thumbs and fingertips from

their gloves. This simple trick allows them to manipulate their line, rod, and reel more easily.

When you are ice fishing for speckled trout on an unfamiliar lake, look for beaver houses. They attract baitfish, which in turn attract speckles. Their brush houses are found in water 6 to 12 feet (1.8 to 3.6 m) deep and may show through the surface of the ice.

- Take a gaff along during your ice-fishing trip. Some of the biggest fish are caught during the winter months, and it would be a real shame to lose one at the rim of the hole while trying to grasp it with your hands.

- Twigs with lines tied to them work well as extra ice-fishing rigs. Always choose flexible branches that are 2 to 3 feet (60 cm to 90 cm) in length. Dogwood and willow are best. Anchor the stem of the twig close to the hole with ice and snow. Wet the base and let it freeze. Make sure the branch is at a 45-degree angle over the hole. Tie a line to the twig, bait it, and you're ready to watch it bend when the fish begin to bite.

- Spring flag tip-ups work well, but make sure the reel spool doesn't freeze if it is left out of the water for a long period of time. Always test the spool before submersing it in the hole.

- Cautious ice fishermen will look for dark spots that signal weak ice areas when venturing onto the ice early and late in the season.

- Many sporting goods stores sell slip-on ice spikes called ice creepers. They're very efficient on the ice, helping you cross the most slippery surfaces.

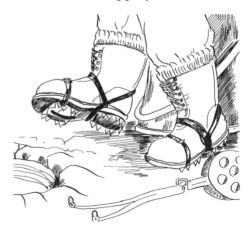

▽

Whether you go on foot or use a snow machine, children's sleds are great for hauling your equipment out onto the ice.

A first-aid kit is a must on a winter fishing trip, yet a survival kit is even better. Include these items in a small bag: handkerchief, wool socks, space blanket, self-sealing plastic bags, whistle, waterproof matches, instant tea or coffee, bouillon cubes, granola bars, a few hard candies, a piece of aluminum foil to use as a signal if you become stranded on the ice, and a sharp knife.

A good way to keep your catch fresh until you have finished fishing is to cut an extra hole. Put your fish on a stringer, drop them through the hole, and tie the stringer to your minnow bucket.

If you have the least bit of doubt about ice thickness, cut a pole and carry it as if you were a tightrope walker. If you crack through the ice, the pole will enable you to climb out of the water.

Here are some guidelines for traveling over ice of different thicknesses:
- *1 to 2 inches (2.5 to 5 cm)* — Unsafe.
- *3 inches (7 cm)* — Will hold a few anglers but they must be spread out.
- *4 inches (10 cm)* — Safe for general use.
- *5 inches (12 cm)* — Snowmobiles can be used.
- *8 to 12 inches (20 to 30 cm)* — Cars and/or light trucks can be used.

Always take an extra pair of gloves or mitts on the ice with you. It's common to get your gloves wet when fighting and landing a fish.

- A quick way to warm up your hands is to place them under your armpits. Also be sure to dry your hands every time they get wet.

- A good way to warm up your hands and/or feet while fishing is to use charcoal briquettes in a coffee can. First place a few holes in the can to create air flow. Then put a little sand in the bottom of the can and top it with a layer of briquettes. The glowing coals will provide heat for hours.

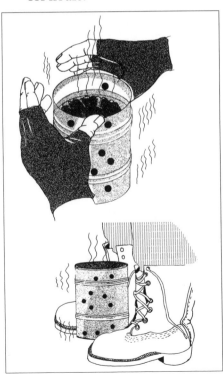

- Cold feet can ruin ice-fishing trips. To keep your feet warm, wear two pairs of socks — a light cotton pair with a heavier wool pair on top.

- Heat-saving inner soles can be made from the Styrofoam trays used to package meat. Just trace the outline of each foot on a tray, trim the excess Styrofoam away, and place the new inner soles into your boots.

- If you ice fish and don't have a hut, you can stay warm by sitting on a simple seat-heater. To make one, use a wooden crate, such as the ones used for holding pop bottles, invert it, and attach it with hinges to a small sled or toboggan. Place a catalytic heater inside the crate. The box can also double as an all-purpose storage box.

Boating

Many anglers who own boats, big or small, spend at least part of the off-season designing more efficient ways to store their rods, lures, and other accessories in their vessels.

There's no question that if your fishing gear is well stored on your boat, you'll enjoy more productive fishing time on the water. However, all boats also need to carry proper safety equipment and should be kept in good operating order. Fishing from boats should be safe as well as fun whether you fish from a canoe, a small motorboat, an inflatable, or a luxury cruiser.

◄ You can turn your aluminum boat into a bass boat by making your own front-casting platform. Cut a thin piece of plywood to fit the front of your boat and fill the open space below it with expanding foam.

◄ If you add floorboards to your aluminum boat, you can store your tackle boxes easily without having them slide into the center of the boat every time you go through rough water. The flooring also makes standing much easier while you're fishing.

◄ Gluing an old bicycle inner tube to the gunwale of the boat provides a handy rod rest that won't scratch your rod.

◄ Keep an extra ignition key for your boat on your car key ring. This will prevent disappointment if you accidentally leave your boat keys at home.

◄ A good place to keep an extra boat key is under your boat dash or in a non-locking compartment. Just tape it in a place that no one will see.

◄ Losing the boat keys can ruin your entire fishing trip. Floating key chains are available at most marinas. To make one, simply run the key chain through a

Many anglers store their tackle boxes inside boat compartments to keep them out of the way. Never, however, put them in your live well. The well can become cracked, which will lead to leaks. When storing your tackle boxes in fiberglass boat compartments, line the compartments with carpet to prevent scratches and cracks to both the compartments and the tackle boxes.

Always consult hydrographic maps for lakes you are planning to fish. Numerous engines and boat hulls are damaged every year by boaters who don't take the time to learn about the bottom contours of lakes.

Never try to go through a lock by yourself, especially if you own an expensive boat. The jostling and bumping that can occur in a crowded lock will leave permanent marks on your boat if there are not enough hands to protect your valuable investment.

One of the easiest items to lose is your boat's drain plug. Two handy spots to keep it are on your engine's kill switch cord and in the splash well. Keeping the plug in a consistent location will help you keep track of it.

hook eye and screw a cork onto the hook.

You can make your own rod tie-downs by sewing Velcro fasteners onto old seat-belt webbing and attaching the straps to your boat seats or deck.

If you have to dock your boat and you don't have bumpers to protect your valuable investment, simply tie the mooring ropes through your life jackets to give the needed protection.

You can make an inexpensive extension to your trolling motor handle with PVC pipe. Fasten a piece of pipe to the handle with a simple hose clamp.

If you frequently fish in windy conditions, carry two anchors aboard your boat. When you anchor both ends of the boat, you don't have to suffer the frustration of a boat that swings back and forth, especially if you're fishing a defined weed line or shoal.

One of the best garbage containers to use in a boat is an old tennis ball can. You can use it for discarding fishing line or ruined plastic baits while out on the water. The can also doubles as a bailer should the need arise.

One of the handiest "extra" items to have stored on a boat is plastic garbage bags. They can be used to carry fish to be cleaned, can be made into an instant rain poncho, and can also cover up cameras and extra clothing in a sudden downpour.

You should always have a few inexpensive marker buoys on your boat for emergency uses. Simply tie a 30-foot (9-m) length of heavy monofilament line to a piece of scrap wood and a heavy lead weight or some bell sinkers. These instant marker buoys can be tossed overboard if you drop something in the water. You can come back later with a diving mask to look for the lost item. Marker buoys are also great for marking a fishing hot spot.

When you need a marker quickly, a bumper cushion works well. Adding a weight to one end will make it stand up and become even more visible in the water.

Another simple marker buoy can be made from a screw-top plastic jug. Just tie on about 25 feet (7.5 m) of line and use a heavy sinker as the weight.

By cleaning the algae, dirt, and grime from your boat's hull several times each season, your boat's performance, speed, and fuel efficiency will stay right on track.

Microphone clips for your CB or VHF radio are sometimes a bother. Velcro strips work much better, making your microphone easier to handle.

Placing some 1-inch (2.5-cm) thick sheets of Styrofoam in an unused storage box on your boat converts it into an excellent ice chest. Just glue the pieces together with RTV silicone, leaving the drain plug uncovered for proper drainage.

• A good boater should use courtesy, common sense, and safety at all times.

• The best way to prevent mildew is ventilation. Careful drying and cleaning of all surfaces and fabrics after each fishing trip is a must.

• More and more anglers have started using hydrographic maps. Much valuable information can be obtained from these maps, including variable water depths, weed lines, shoals, and other underwater contours. Maps can be purchased from many tackle stores and governmental fisheries authorities.

• There are many ways to protect your boating and hydrographic maps. Here's a good one. Cover the surfaces with transparent contact sheeting. These plastic materials are self-adhesive and can be purchased in most department or hardware stores. To further protect them, keep the maps rolled up at home in a PVC pipe or cardboard tube with both ends capped.

• To keep your map open for viewing, yet protected from water, place it flat on the dash. Purchase a piece of Plexiglas to hold the map in place. Use two long strips of Velcro to hold the Plexiglas to the dash.

◄ Tossing an anchor or dropping heavy objects inside your boat will frighten the fish.

◄ Many anglers forget about their stringer when traveling from spot to spot. If you hang it from the forward part of the boat, you'll see your catch flopping about and be able to pull them into the boat. At the front of the boat they will also stay clear of the prop .

◄ For a good-looking boat finish, use furniture polish in a spray can. The dirt and grime will float off with a spray from your water hose.

◄ Rods and reels can get battered when they are bounced around in a boat. Hardware departments carry clips for broom handles, which can be attached to your boat and used to keep your rods standing upright while the boat is moving. Rod holders can also be made from plastic pipe.

◄ Many anglers make their own boat anchors. Check at your local truck service center or auto parts specialty house for a broken truck axle shaft. All you have to do is weld a big nut onto the end of the shaft and you've got yourself an 8-pound (3.5-kg) anchor.

Zebra mussels are rapidly becoming a major problem in many North American lakes. It's important to clean your boat hull thoroughly and rinse your linewells and bilge out before trailering to another lake. Also, make sure you remove all weeds clinging to your boat, outboard motor, or trailer when traveling from one spot to another. This conservation practice helps prevent undesirable weeds from being introduced to other waters. In many areas, it's also the law.

A cheap yet durable anchor can be made from a plastic bleach bottle. Fill it with sand, screw the cap back on, attach an anchor rope through its handle, and it's ready for use.

One of the key characteristics missing in some fishing boats is a good-sized cockpit. Look for a boat with a lot of open space for storage and moving around in.

If you want to improve the fuel efficiency and top-end speed of your high-performance boat, try using a jack plate. This metal plate is attached to the back of the boat between the motor and the boat. Most are fully adjustable, allowing you to change the position of the motor for maximum performance.

The worst item to use to cover your outboard motor over the winter is a plastic sheet. Not only will it hold moisture, but it can also scratch your paint finish. Use an old sheet or large cloth to keep the dust out and the fresh air in.

Small squares of sample carpeting are available from most rug centers at very cheap prices. They can be used to deaden noise, especially in aluminum boats. You can place them under tackle boxes, ice chests, gas tanks, even in anchor storage areas.

Your boat may travel a little too fast for a particular species. A sea anchor or even a plastic bucket will help slow down the speed of your boat. Drop it about 10 feet (3 m) behind the boat.

Owners of aluminum boats can take a handy tip from bass boat anglers. You can rig a couple of homemade bunks covered in carpet onto your trailer; this will allow you to drive your boat right up onto the trailer.

High-performance boaters should invest in a foot throttle. It's much safer than a hand throttle, especially in rough seas.

Purchasing a motor that is over 10 hp in size may not necessarily be the right way to go. Don't forget, you're going to have to load this heavy motor onto your boat, carry it certain distances, and also have it registered. In almost every case, a 5- to 9.9-hp motor will more than do the job for a 12- to 16-foot (3.6- to 4.8-m) aluminum boat.

Trim your outboard motor out if the bow is too low and it crashes into oncoming waves. Trim your outboard in if your bow is too high and it causes the boat to "porpoise."

Make sure you mix your gasoline and oil as recommended by your manufacturer. You'll find that the motor will run more smoothly, start more easily, and have a longer life.

- Electric outboards are ideal for fishing shallow waters, can be operated at very slow speeds over weed lines, and are efficient and quiet.

- Always strap your batteries down. Heavy batteries can bounce up and down in rough water, causing damage to the floor of your boat and even your hull from the constant pounding.

- Good batteries can be a sizable investment for your boat, especially if you are running a trolling motor. To extend the life of your batteries, remember these tips:

• Always check the water levels in each cell of the battery before charging.
• Use a wire brush to clean the terminals every couple of months.
• Don't use high amperage battery chargers; anything over 20 amps will decrease the life of your battery.
• Try to run the battery almost all the way down before you charge it or it will never maintain a full charge.
• Make sure you charge your batteries before you store them for the winter and charge them every month to keep up a full charge.
• Make sure no fluid is leaking from the batteries if you are carrying them by hand; leaking battery acid will eat your clothing.
• Always use a separate battery or batteries for your trolling motor so you don't risk losing power to crank your engine.

- Canoes should not be used for fishing unless you are an experienced canoeist. They can be dangerous in inexperienced hands.

- Many boaters, especially those who love to fish, travel on the water after dark. To find your way home quickly, attach reflective strips to the end of your dock.

When you're going into a back lake to do some fishing on your own, an anchor for your canoe will probably come in handy. To avoid carrying one in, fold up the mesh from an onion bag in your knapsack. When you arrive at your favorite lake, just place a rock in the bag and attach it to your canoe.

When you are night fishing in a boat, reflector tape strips placed on hard-to-find items — tackle boxes, net handles, gaffs, and boat keys — will help you locate them more quickly.

If by chance you're dumped out of a canoe in heavy rapids, get upstream of the canoe if possible so that the canoe can't ram you. When floating downstream, try to go feet-first so that you can see the current changes and other obstructions such as rocks and boulders.

You can easily ruin your canoe paddle by pushing off docks, shallow water, and rocks with it. Just use the other end, which can take this type of beating.

Crossing a fast-moving stream in a canoe can sometimes be a problem. Just angle your craft a few degrees toward the other shore but upstream. By using this technique, you'll prevent the current from taking you and your canoe a long distance downstream.

Before leaving home with your boat and trailer, check that the wheel nuts are snug; the trailer is securely tightened to the hitch ball and that the safety chains are attached with enough slack; the electrical system is hooked up and working properly; all tie-downs are tight; the winch is locked; and your vehicle's mirrors are adjusted correctly for proper visibility.

Use an old tennis ball as a cover for your trailer hitch ball. Putting a small slit in the tennis ball will allow it to slip easily over the hitch and keep any grease or dirt from getting on your clothing.

One of the biggest headaches when loading a boat on its trailer is lining it up properly on the rollers or bunks. A handy way to simplify this task is to use a couple of the flags mounted on flexible rods that are used on bicycles. They will stick up above the water no matter how far in you back your trailer.

It is very important to attach the back of your boat tightly to the trailer with tie-down straps. On rough roads, a boat can jump several inches (centimeters) in the air leading to a damaged hull, especially on rivetted aluminum boats.

Double check with your insurance company regarding your boat and trailer policy. Make sure you have the type of coverage that will cover you while your boat is stored for the winter, left unattended, or being trailered.

If you own a boat shed or garage, hang a tennis ball from the ceiling about 3 feet (90 cm) off the back wall, low enough so that it bounces off the boat when you back in. This will protect not only your propeller and trailer lights but also the back of your garage.

Before launching a boat, always check your ramp site for obstructions; double check that your drain plug is securely in place and that your trailer lights are disconnected; trim your motor into the up position; and make sure your bow and stern lines are accessible. Always back up your boat slowly.

It is essential to maintain the tire manufacturers' recommended pressure for your trailer tires. Tires that are too soft will overheat and could cause a blowout. Hard tires, although not dangerous, cause a rough ride.

If you constantly have trouble launching your boat from a trailer, install a ball hitch on your vehicle's front bumper. When

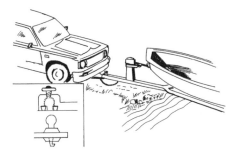

you arrive at the ramp site, unhitch the trailer from its regular position and attach it to the front. You'll gain more control and be able to see exactly where you are going. When you're finished fishing, pick up your boat in the same manner.

Don't pile all your equipment and supplies into the stern of your boat when trailering. It may lift your hitch and cause steering problems, especially on the highway.

Never stand directly in front of a trailer winch line when cranking a boat into position. A parting rope or cable could catapult backwards or a handle could spin, causing serious injury.

Carrying a boat on top of your car can sometimes cause problems. For instance, the ropes holding the boat at the front and back may rub the paint finish off the car. You can prevent this by placing foam-rubber pads where the rope touches the car. The rubber can be held in place by taping the pieces to the rope.

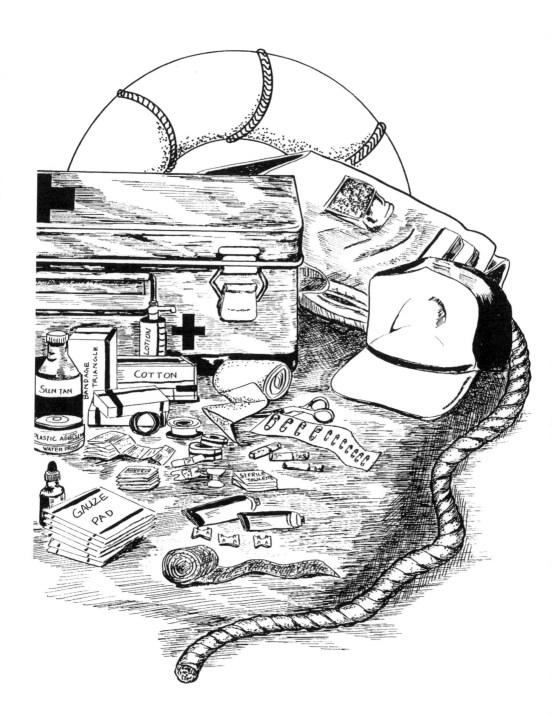

Safety and First Aid

Whether you consider yourself to be an amateur or a professional, safety rules and first aid should be learned and learned well. All anglers, young and old, should practice and promote safety in sportfishing.

It's a good idea to heed the Boy Scouts' motto "Be prepared," because you never know when you will need to administer first aid. You could be wading in a river or fishing in a boat when an accident occurs.

Each year, anglers suffer injuries or even die due to negligence or poor safety practices. To fish safely, keep abreast of weather conditions, be alert to possible accident situations, and understand the basics of first aid.

Always wear an approved life jacket when traveling in a boat. If you fish standing up, make sure your life jacket remains on. Set a good example, especially for children.

On a fishing trip, take along some spare clothing, a flashlight, whistle, knife, first-aid kit, and emergency rations in a watertight plastic bag.

Many small boats are poorly equipped when it comes to safety. The following equipment should be carried on your boat: a first-aid kit, flares, a flashlight, knife, tool kit, water-

proof matches, and a life jacket for everyone aboard.

Before traveling to your fishing spot, it's wise to remove lures or hooks from your rod. This is not only a good safety measure, but also a time-saving tip. You won't have to spend time removing hooks from your upholstery when you arrive.

Many boating accidents occur every year. These tips can save your life:
- Don't go too far from shore on large bodies of water if you're in a small boat.
- Any drastic changes in weather

can be dangerous; take all necessary precautions in inclement weather.

- Ensure that your boat is safety-equipped according to its size.
- Make sure everyone aboard is wearing a life jacket.
- Watch your alcohol intake when fishing and abstain when operating a boat. It's illegal to operate a boat under the influence of alcohol.

 Many fishermen drown each year in boating accidents. Rescuing others requires a little instruction. Try to use a fishing rod, paddle, rope, or even your jacket to reach the accident victim. Brace yourself, then when he grabs on, pull him in. Use a boat to rescue the victim when he's too far to reach from shore.

Many boats have exploded during the fueling process. Remember to shut off the engine and any other electrical device capable of producing a spark. Close all hatches and windows so that the fumes can't blow inside. Passengers should not smoke in the fueling area. All portable fuel tanks should be removed from the boat and filled on shore.

Keep safe when boating on the water. If your boat goes over 30 miles (48 km) an hour, you might want to invest in a used motorcycle helmet for rainy weather. The visor will protect you if you have to run at top speed in the pelting rain to get off the lake.

- Remember that port is left and starboard is right. Follow proper boating regulations, and be alert to changing weather conditions at all times.

- A bailing can should be aboard every type of boat. You never know when your automatic or manual bilge pump may break down. To make a bailer from a plastic bleach bottle, cut off the bottom, leave the cap on the top portion, and you have a bailing can with a handle.

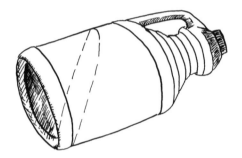

- Flashlight batteries should be checked before every trip. If an emergency occurs, it would be a shame if the batteries were dead.

- While fishing, many anglers forget about skin damage from overexposure to the sun. Be sure to use the proper sunscreen for your skin type and to gradually tan rather than try to get a tan all in one day. Wear a wide-brimmed hat or cap, and if you're spending a long day on the water, wear a long-sleeved, light-colored shirt as well. At the end of the day, a skin moisturizer should be used.

- If your boat has a top, by all means put it up when you're spending a number of hours fishing on the lake. You can never get enough protection from the damaging rays of the sun.

- Stinging insects are bothersome throughout the fishing season. If you do get stung, you should remove the stinger if there is one. Apply a paste of baking soda and water on ant and bee stings. Mosquito and blackfly bites can be soothed by applying calamine lotion.

- Even pro fishermen accidentally hook themselves. When medical help is not available, these procedures will help you remove most hooks. Run a sterilized blunt needle down the path of the hook and rotate it until it's on the barb side of the hook. Back out the hook, using the end of the needle as support. Next, wash the area well and dab the wound with an antiseptic solution. Place a bandage over the cut to prevent any infection.

Here's another widely used method to remove an embedded hook. Attach a loop of heavy fishing line to the hook

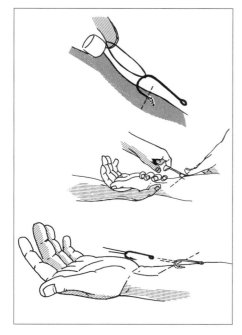

bend, quickly and lightly depress the hook with your thumb, and sharply jerk on the loop to remove the hook.

If by chance you get a slight burn from a campfire, apply cold water or ice for ten minutes or so. You should then apply burn ointment or a baking soda paste and put a light bandage over it.

Be careful when crossing obstructions such as fences, especially when you're wearing waders and carrying your fishing equipment. A seemingly simple task like this may result in a puncture in your waders, a broken rod, or even an unfortunate accident.

Be alert to rising waters if you have to make a trip back across a stream. Heavy rains and tides can change water depths by up to 3 feet (90 cm).

To help prevent insect bites, you should wear light-colored clothing, long-sleeved shirts, full-length pants, and a good insect repellent.

Be careful when you cast. A back-whip action could hook someone. A double check around you before you cast could prevent an accident.

Whenever you are using chest waders, always wear a snug wading belt around your waist. If you do fall in, the belt will prevent water from filling your waders and eventually pulling you under.

Cleaning and Cooking Fish

Although each type of fish has its own flavor, texture, and appearance, the basic rules for cleaning and cooking fish are the same.

If you plan to do a lot of fishing and you enjoy eating fish, it's important to take steps to make sure your catch will taste as fresh as possible at the table. Many anglers don't clean their fish properly before storing them. Improper cleaning takes some of the flavor out of the fish and leaves many broken bones inside. Filleting is by far the best method of cleaning your catch, and with a little practice, anyone can master the technique.

Sportfishing is enjoyable and relaxing — your dinner can be, too!

add a couple of drops of vanilla extract. Leave the lid open for a few hours so the air can circulate. An electric fan directed at the interior will increase the flow of air and speed up the deodorizing process.

- Caviar is made from the eggs of certain fish, but do not use the eggs of pike, which are considered toxic to humans.

- Normark's mesh fillet glove will help you clean spiny fish such as bass and panfish.

- Many anglers like to camp and fish on back lakes. It's easy to make a skillet — better than hauling one. Bend a wire coat hanger into the form of a circle with a handle. Cover the circle with a double layer of aluminum foil, crimping it over the edges to make yourself a frying pan.

- Always trim the fatty tissue around the bellies of fish before cooking them. This will make the fish tastier.

- Fish are usually cut in fillets or steaks for cooking. Try oven cooking whole small fish in foil with some onion and fresh parsley.

- Never freeze fish without cleaning them, except in the winter when it is cold enough to freeze them solid as soon as they are out of the water.

- When you catch a fish and want it to hold its shape, freeze it on a board.

- To avoid the smell of fish in the freezer, wrap your catch in a double layer of newspaper.

- To get rid of persistent odors in the freezer, wash it with baking soda and lukewarm water, then

◄ When you clean your catch, instead of tossing the remains into the garbage can, use them as fertilizer. Bury them around your bushes and flowers. Not only will your flowers smell sweeter, but so will your garbage.

◄ Fish caught in warm, weedy, mud-bottomed lakes taste better if they are skinned, whereas fish caught in cold, clear water are fine scaled.

◄ To kill the odor left on your hands after cleaning fish, wash them first with salt and then with soap.

◄ When cooking fish over a fire, make a small fire that burns intensely. Don't use wet or green wood, which creates a lot of smoke but not much heat.

◄ In order to preserve the flavor of your catch, the fish should be cleaned as soon as possible and frozen or kept cool on ice.

◄ If you are on a backpacking or canoe trip and want to take your catch home, don't kill the fish right away. Try to keep them alive on a stringer in the water until you're ready to leave.

◄ Here are some guidelines for keeping your catch fresh: remove slime and scale fish as soon as possible; immediately bleed the fish (cut the fish behind the gills on the belly side); remove the intestines (digestive enzymes of feeding fish are so active that they'll continue their activity and begin to digest the fish itself); remove the dark streak along the backbone (the kidney), cut the covering membrane, and scrape it out with a spoon (it also is a chief source of flavor-destroying enzymes); lastly, remove the head to save some cooler and freezer space.

HOW TO FILLET A FISH

• Make the first cut just behind the gills. Slice down to the bone, then, without removing the blade, turn it and slice straight along the backbone.

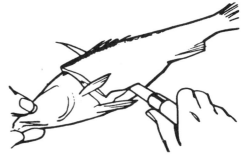

• Continue slicing to the tail. Note that the fillet has been cut away from the rest of the fish.

After slicing the fillet off at the tail, turn the fish over and repeat the procedure on the other side.

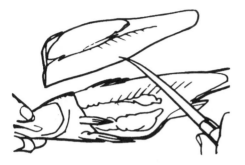

• With both sides removed, you have cut away both fillets without disturbing the fish's entrails. This is the neatest and fastest way to prepare fish.

• The next step is to remove the rib section. A sharp, flexible knife is important to avoid wasting meat. Insert the blade close to the rib bones and slice the

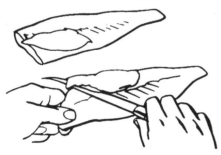

entire section away. This should be done before the skin is removed to keep waste to a minimum.

• Removing the skin from each fillet is simply a matter of inserting a knife at the tail and cutting the meat from the skin. Start the cut ½ inch (1.2 cm) from the tail end of the skin.

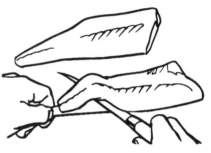

• Each fillet is now ready for the pan or freezer. Remember not to overwash the fillets in order to retain the juices and keep the meat in its firm natural state.

• Cutting out the "cheeks" is the next important step. Few fishermen know that the cheeks are the filet mignon of the fish. Though small, they're tasty and well worth saving.

- Slice into the cheek where indicated, then scoop out the meat with the blade, peeling away the skin. Repeat on the other side. Many fishermen save the cheeks until they have accumulated enough for a real gourmet's delight.

- Never leave fresh fish soaking in water. Wash the fish quickly, drain, and dry carefully. Don't overcook your catch, and turn it only once during cooking.

- An excellent method for cooking fish is barbecuing. Both steaks and fillets can be cooked in this manner. Don't forget to dab the fish with paper towels before cooking. Place the fish onto double foil pads, cut to the size of your grill. Baste frequently with a lemon-butter mixture and test with a fork. The meat is done when it flakes.

- Some gamefish, such as largemouth bass and pike, have a strong-tasting flesh in the lateral line area. This dark-colored flesh along the side of a fish should be removed if you plan to freeze your catch for more than one month.

- A good way to prepare fish for the refrigerator is to wipe fillets, whole fish, or steaks with paper towels, then place them on paper towels, and cover them tightly with a stretch plastic wrap.

- When pan-frying, an easy way to check if your fish is thoroughly cooked is to insert a fork through the backbone section and twist. The flesh will separate easily from the bone when it is done.

- Here's a good rule of thumb for steaking fish. Fish over 10 pounds (4.5 kg) should be steaked or chunked so they are easier to cook. Remember to trim and throw away the fatty tissue around the bellies of the steak ends.

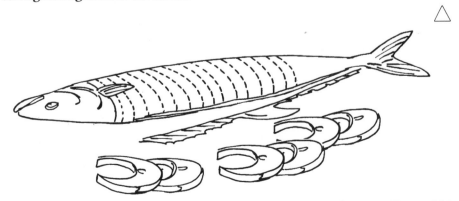

The best way to keep your catch fresh is to place it in a cooler that is filled to the brim with cracked or crushed ice.

There's nothing like a shore lunch. Even when your catch is too small for filleting, it will be just right for pan-frying. Clean the cavity, leaving the head, fins, and tail intact. Wipe each fish with a dry paper towel, roll it in flour and seasoning, and you're ready to go. Melt a little butter over a medium hot fire and brown your fish in it for six to ten minutes.

By attaching your fish to a log or board with a knife, nail, or another sharp object, you can easily fillet or scale it without having it slip and move around.

For tasty fried fish, always sear the outside over high heat. This will help to retain moisture and most of the flavor in the flesh as it is cooking.

Many anglers have turned to microwave cooking. Lean fish should be microwaved at 100 percent power and oily fish at 50 percent. The meat of fattier fish tends to separate at higher settings.

If you aren't sure if the fish you have caught is spoiled, check its ribs. If the ribs detach easily from the flesh, the fish is starting to spoil.

Whether you're thawing whole or cut fillets, place the fish in a shallow pan and pour enough fresh milk over it to cover the fish completely. People who use this method say the milk seems to restore the fresh-caught flavor.

The flesh of fish carries many tasty juices, much like that of good meat. Remember to wash your fillets in cold water and with as little force as possible. This will help retain the juices.

Instead of buying ice for storing your fish, freeze large blocks of ice at home. Take milk bags that don't leak, fill them with water, seal them with a twist tie, and freeze them. Put six to eight in your cooler and they will keep for one or two days.

◆ Thoroughly washed milk cartons make excellent containers for freezing your catch. Just make sure your fish are covered with water in the container. Date the carton and place a piece of foil on top before freezing.

◆ To remove the strong taste of some fish, let the fish soak in beaten eggs in a bowl. The longer the fish soaks, the milder it will taste.

◆ When filleting walleyes, cut out the cheeks and fry them. Many people consider them a gourmet treat. They taste like fried scallops.

◆ Fish spoil quickly without air circulation, so don't use non-porous wrappings such as plastic garbage bags for holding fish before you freeze them. Ice coolers, burlap bags, and newspapers are better.

◆ Never transport fish in the trunk of a car or on the back seat. Always take a cooler and some ice along on a fishing trip and gut and store the fish as soon as you catch it.

◆ When preparing a shore lunch, a paddle works well if you have nowhere else to fillet your fish.

◆ Specially designed scissors, such as the ones from Normark Industries, will help you clean your catch. They're ideal for gilling and gutting trout in the field and for cleaning smelt, perch, and other small fish.

Fishing Log

DATE	FISHING LOCATION	HOURS FISHED

SUNRISE	MOON PHASE	SUNSET
AM		PM

WIND CONDITIONS

WIND	N	E	S	W	NE	NW	SE	SW	WIND	N	E	S	W	NE	NW	SE	SW
AM									PM								

WEATHER CONDITIONS

SKY	❑ CLEAR	❑ PARTLY CLOUDY	❑ CLOUDY
PRECIPITATION	❑ DRIZZLE	❑ RAIN	❑ SNOW
VARIABLES	❑ COLD FRONT	❑ FOG	❑ OTHER
BAROMETER	❑ STEADY	❑ RISING	❑ FALLING

WATER CONDITIONS

WATER CLARITY	❑ DIRTY	❑ STAINED	❑ CLEAR
WATER CURRENT	❑ FAST	❑ MODERATE	❑ SLOW
WATER LEVEL	❑ HIGH	❑ NORMAL	❑ LOW
WATER SURFACE	❑ ROUGH	❑ CHOPPY	❑ CALM
SURFACE TEMPERATURE		AM	PM
TEMPERATURE AT LURE DEPTH		AM	PM
THERMOCLINE RANGE		HIGH	LOW

TIME CAUGHT	AM	PM	SPECIES
			LURE
LENGTH	IN	CM	MODEL
WEIGHT	LB	OZ	COLOR AND SIZE
		KG	RETRIEVE DESCRIPTION
DEPTH CAUGHT		FT / M	RIVER/LAKE LOCATION
LINE WEIGHT		LB	❑ MUD ❑ GRAVEL ❑ BOULDERS
LINE TYPE			❑ SAND ❑ ROCKS ❑ BREAKWATER
LOCATION CAUGHT			

RIVER/LAKE LOCATION

❑ MUD	❑ GRAVEL	❑ BOULDERS
❑ SAND	❑ ROCKS	❑ BREAKWATER
❑ WEEDS	❑ PADS	❑ BRUSH
❑ REEDS	❑ WEED LINE	❑ STUMPS
❑ RAPIDS	❑ DAM	❑ ABUTMENT
❑ EDDIES	❑ SLICK WATER	❑ HOLDING POOL
❑ SLOPING	❑ DROP-OFF	❑ DOCKS
❑ FLAT	❑ HUMP	❑ OTHER

TIME CAUGHT	AM	PM	SPECIES		
			LURE		
LENGTH	IN	CM	MODEL		
WEIGHT	LB	OZ	COLOR AND SIZE		
		KG	RETRIEVE DESCRIPTION		
DEPTH CAUGHT		FT M	RIVER/LAKE LOCATION		
LINE WEIGHT		LB	❏ MUD	❏ GRAVEL	❏ BOULDERS
			❏ SAND	❏ ROCKS	❏ BREAKWATER
LINE TYPE			❏ WEEDS	❏ PADS	❏ BRUSH
			❏ REEDS	❏ WEED LINE	❏ STUMPS
LOCATION CAUGHT			❏ RAPIDS	❏ DAM	❏ ABUTMENT
			❏ EDDIES	❏ SLICK WATER	❏ HOLDING POOL
			❏ SLOPING	❏ DROP-OFF	❏ DOCKS
			❏ FLAT	❏ HUMP	❏ OTHER

TIME CAUGHT	AM	PM	SPECIES		
			LURE		
LENGTH	IN	CM	MODEL		
WEIGHT	LB	OZ	COLOR AND SIZE		
		KG	RETRIEVE DESCRIPTION		
DEPTH CAUGHT		FT M	RIVER/LAKE LOCATION		
LINE WEIGHT		LB	❏ MUD	❏ GRAVEL	❏ BOULDERS
			❏ SAND	❏ ROCKS	❏ BREAKWATER
LINE TYPE			❏ WEEDS	❏ PADS	❏ BRUSH
			❏ REEDS	❏ WEED LINE	❏ STUMPS
LOCATION CAUGHT			❏ RAPIDS	❏ DAM	❏ ABUTMENT
			❏ EDDIES	❏ SLICK WATER	❏ HOLDING POOL
			❏ SLOPING	❏ DROP-OFF	❏ DOCKS
			❏ FLAT	❏ HUMP	❏ OTHER

NOTES _____

_____

_____

_____

_____

_____

DATE		FISHING LOCATION	HOURS FISHED

SUNRISE		MOON PHASE	SUNSET
AM			PM

WIND CONDITIONS

WIND	N	E	S	W	NE	NW	SE	SW	WIND	N	E	S	W	NE	NW	SE	SW
AM									PM								

WEATHER CONDITIONS

SKY	❑ CLEAR	❑ PARTLY CLOUDY	❑ CLOUDY
PRECIPITATION	❑ DRIZZLE	❑ RAIN	❑ SNOW
VARIABLES	❑ COLD FRONT	❑ FOG	❑ OTHER
BAROMETER	❑ STEADY	❑ RISING	❑ FALLING

WATER CONDITIONS

WATER CLARITY	❑ DIRTY	❑ STAINED	❑ CLEAR
WATER CURRENT	❑ FAST	❑ MODERATE	❑ SLOW
WATER LEVEL	❑ HIGH	❑ NORMAL	❑ LOW
WATER SURFACE	❑ ROUGH	❑ CHOPPY	❑ CALM
SURFACE TEMPERATURE		AM	PM
TEMPERATURE AT LURE DEPTH		AM	PM
THERMOCLINE RANGE		HIGH	LOW

TIME	AM	PM	SPECIES
CAUGHT			LURE
LENGTH	IN	CM	MODEL
WEIGHT	LB	OZ	COLOR AND SIZE
		KG	RETRIEVE DESCRIPTION
DEPTH		FT	RIVER/LAKE LOCATION
CAUGHT		M	❑ MUD ❑ GRAVEL ❑ BOULDERS
LINE		LB	❑ SAND ❑ ROCKS ❑ BREAKWATER
WEIGHT			❑ WEEDS ❑ PADS ❑ BRUSH
LINE			❑ REEDS ❑ WEED LINE ❑ STUMPS
TYPE			❑ RAPIDS ❑ DAM ❑ ABUTMENT
LOCATION CAUGHT			❑ EDDIES ❑ SLICK WATER ❑ HOLDING POOL
			❑ SLOPING ❑ DROP-OFF ❑ DOCKS
			❑ FLAT ❑ HUMP ❑ OTHER

TIME CAUGHT	AM	PM	SPECIES
			LURE
LENGTH	IN	CM	MODEL
WEIGHT	LB	OZ	COLOR AND SIZE
		KG	RETRIEVE DESCRIPTION

DEPTH CAUGHT		FT M	RIVER/LAKE LOCATION
LINE WEIGHT		LB	❏ MUD ❏ GRAVEL ❏ BOULDERS
			❏ SAND ❏ ROCKS ❏ BREAKWATER
LINE TYPE			❏ WEEDS ❏ PADS ❏ BRUSH
			❏ REEDS ❏ WEED LINE ❏ STUMPS
LOCATION CAUGHT			❏ RAPIDS ❏ DAM ❏ ABUTMENT
			❏ EDDIES ❏ SLICK WATER ❏ HOLDING POOL
			❏ SLOPING ❏ DROP-OFF ❏ DOCKS
			❏ FLAT ❏ HUMP ❏ OTHER

TIME CAUGHT	AM	PM	SPECIES
			LURE
LENGTH	IN	CM	MODEL
WEIGHT	LB	OZ	COLOR AND SIZE
		KG	RETRIEVE DESCRIPTION

DEPTH CAUGHT		FT M	RIVER/LAKE LOCATION
LINE WEIGHT		LB	❏ MUD ❏ GRAVEL ❏ BOULDERS
			❏ SAND ❏ ROCKS ❏ BREAKWATER
LINE TYPE			❏ WEEDS ❏ PADS ❏ BRUSH
			❏ REEDS ❏ WEED LINE ❏ STUMPS
LOCATION CAUGHT			❏ RAPIDS ❏ DAM ❏ ABUTMENT
			❏ EDDIES ❏ SLICK WATER ❏ HOLDING POOL
			❏ SLOPING ❏ DROP-OFF ❏ DOCKS
			❏ FLAT ❏ HUMP ❏ OTHER

NOTES _____

_____

_____

_____

_____

_____

DATE							FISHING LOCATION					HOURS FISHED					
SUNRISE							MOON PHASE					SUNSET					
AM														PM			

WIND CONDITIONS

WIND	N	E	S	W	NE	NW	SE	SW	WIND	N	E	S	W	NE	NW	SE	SW
AM									PM								

WEATHER CONDITIONS

SKY	❏ CLEAR	❏ PARTLY CLOUDY	❏ CLOUDY
PRECIPITATION	❏ DRIZZLE	❏ RAIN	❏ SNOW
VARIABLES	❏ COLD FRONT	❏ FOG	❏ OTHER
BAROMETER	❏ STEADY	❏ RISING	❏ FALLING

WATER CONDITIONS

WATER CLARITY	❏ DIRTY	❏ STAINED	❏ CLEAR
WATER CURRENT	❏ FAST	❏ MODERATE	❏ SLOW
WATER LEVEL	❏ HIGH	❏ NORMAL	❏ LOW
WATER SURFACE	❏ ROUGH	❏ CHOPPY	❏ CALM
SURFACE TEMPERATURE		AM	PM
TEMPERATURE AT LURE DEPTH		AM	PM
THERMOCLINE RANGE		HIGH	LOW

TIME	AM	PM	SPECIES
CAUGHT			LURE
LENGTH	IN	CM	MODEL
WEIGHT	LB	OZ	COLOR AND SIZE
		KG	RETRIEVE DESCRIPTION
DEPTH		FT	RIVER/LAKE LOCATION
CAUGHT		M	❏ MUD ❏ GRAVEL ❏ BOULDERS
LINE		LB	❏ SAND ❏ ROCKS ❏ BREAKWATER
WEIGHT			❏ WEEDS ❏ PADS ❏ BRUSH
LINE			❏ REEDS ❏ WEED LINE ❏ STUMPS
TYPE			❏ RAPIDS ❏ DAM ❏ ABUTMENT
LOCATION CAUGHT			❏ EDDIES ❏ SLICK WATER ❏ HOLDING POOL
			❏ SLOPING ❏ DROP-OFF ❏ DOCKS
			❏ FLAT ❏ HUMP ❏ OTHER

TIME CAUGHT	AM	PM	SPECIES
			LURE
LENGTH	IN	CM	MODEL
WEIGHT	LB	OZ	COLOR AND SIZE
		KG	RETRIEVE DESCRIPTION

DEPTH CAUGHT FT / M
LINE WEIGHT LB
LINE TYPE
LOCATION CAUGHT

RIVER/LAKE LOCATION

❑ MUD ❑ GRAVEL ❑ BOULDERS
❑ SAND ❑ ROCKS ❑ BREAKWATER
❑ WEEDS ❑ PADS ❑ BRUSH
❑ REEDS ❑ WEED LINE ❑ STUMPS
❑ RAPIDS ❑ DAM ❑ ABUTMENT
❑ EDDIES ❑ SLICK WATER ❑ HOLDING POOL
❑ SLOPING ❑ DROP-OFF ❑ DOCKS
❑ FLAT ❑ HUMP ❑ OTHER

TIME CAUGHT	AM	PM	SPECIES
			LURE
LENGTH	IN	CM	MODEL
WEIGHT	LB	OZ	COLOR AND SIZE
		KG	RETRIEVE DESCRIPTION

DEPTH CAUGHT FT / M
LINE WEIGHT LB
LINE TYPE
LOCATION CAUGHT

RIVER/LAKE LOCATION

❑ MUD ❑ GRAVEL ❑ BOULDERS
❑ SAND ❑ ROCKS ❑ BREAKWATER
❑ WEEDS ❑ PADS ❑ BRUSH
❑ REEDS ❑ WEED LINE ❑ STUMPS
❑ RAPIDS ❑ DAM ❑ ABUTMENT
❑ EDDIES ❑ SLICK WATER ❑ HOLDING POOL
❑ SLOPING ❑ DROP-OFF ❑ DOCKS
❑ FLAT ❑ HUMP ❑ OTHER

NOTES

Index